THE 100+ SERIES™

Reproducible Activities

Using the Standards

Building Grammar & Writing Skills

Grades 7-8

By

Ruth Fennick and Elaine Dion

Published by Instructional Fair • TS Denison
an imprint of

 **Children's Publishing**

Authors: Ruth Fennick and Elaine Dion
Editors: Jerry Aten

 **Children's Publishing**

Published by Instructional Fair • TS Denison
An imprint of McGraw-Hill Children's Publishing
Copyright © 2003 McGraw-Hill Children's Publishing

Send all inquiries to:
McGraw-Hill Children's Publishing
3195 Wilson Drive NW
Grand Rapids, Michigan 49544

Using the Standards: Building Grammar & Writing Skills—grade 7-8
ISBN: 0-7424-1807-3

3 4 5 6 7 8 9 PHXBK 08 07 06 05 04

The *McGraw-Hill* Companies

Introduction

This book provides language and writing activities to help students achieve the goals outlined in the IRA/NCTE *Standards for the English Language Arts* (1996). These standards, addressing all types of language activities (reading, writing, speaking, listening, viewing, and visually representing (have as their overriding goal "to ensure that all students are knowledgeable and proficient users of language that they may succeed in school, participate in our democracy as informed citizens, find challenging and rewarding work, appreciate and contribute to our culture, and pursue their own goals and interests as independent learners." Because this book focuses on grammar and writing, it emphasizes the standards most directly applicable. However, since reading and writing are inextricably linked, aspects of all 12 standards are necessarily included.

Part I: Grammar reviews rules of Standard English in capitalization, punctuation, usage, and parts of speech. The standards most applicable to this section are numbers 4 and 6, which focus on students' ability to use the conventions of Standard English to communicate effectively with various audiences, for multiple purposes, in various media. Activities in this section ask students to review the rules, to identify their application in sentences, as well as in the world around them, and to demonstrate understanding of the rules by creating original passages.

Part II: Writing Strategies teaches specific aspects of the writing process. Students learn to use a wide range of resources to generate, plan, revise, and publish their ideas in various forms and forums for various audiences and purposes. Most, if not all, of the standards are reflected in the activities in this section as students practice the skills through writing, speaking, sketching, using technology, designing visually informative texts, and preparing writing pieces for publication.

Part III: Writing Applications invites students to apply what they learn in Parts I and II to larger writing projects. Most of these projects are representative of the types of writing students would realistically be expected to undertake in and out of school as they complete classroom assignments, take standardized tests, apply for part-time jobs, produce documents on the job, and fulfill personal and social goals. Virtually all of the standards are represented in these activities.

The **Table of Contents** identifies the standards most directly related to specific writing activities in the book. However, because individual standards encompass a wide range of objectives, and because the standards themselves are interrelated, specific writing activities reflect only parts of a single standard, but include aspects of several standards. Because the 12 standards collectively reflect overall curricular goals rather than objectives to apply to discrete activities, the standards indicated in the Table of Contents should be seen as representative rather than definitive.

These standards, reflecting what teacher–researchers have concluded students should be able to do with language and how they can best achieve those goals, are the result of considerable research on how students most effectively learn to use language. For landmark research studies supporting the instruction of grammar and writing as it is reflected in the *Standards for the English Language Arts*, see *The Composing Processes of Twelfth Graders* by Janet Emig (Urbana: NCTE, 1971) and *Research on Written Communication: New Directions for Teaching* by George Hillocks, Jr. (Urbana: ERIC, 1986).

The table of contents includes a column in which the number of each standard that applies to a particular activity is indicated. Teachers and parents can use this as an at-a-glance guide to the standard(s) addressed in each activity. In addition, the specific skill in focus for activity is included in the upper right hand corner of that page.

3

English Language Arts Standards

1. Read a wide range of texts.

2. Read a wide range of literature.

3. Apply a variety of strategies to comprehend and interpret texts.

4. Use spoken, written, and visual language to communicate effectively.

5. Use a variety of strategies while writing and use elements of the writing process to communicate.

6. Apply knowledge of language structure and conventions, media techniques, figurative language, and genre to create, critique, and discuss texts.

7. Research issues and interests, pose questions, and gather data to communicate discoveries.

8. Work with a variety of technological and other resources to collect information and to communicate knowledge.

9. Understand and respect the differences in language use across cultures, regions, and social roles.

10. Students whose first language is not English use their first language to develop competencies in English and other content areas.

11. Participate in a variety of literary communities.

12. Use spoken, written, and visual language to accomplish purposes.

© McGraw-Hill Children's Publishing

0-7424-1807-3 *Building Grammar & Writing Skills*

© McGraw-Hill Children's Publishing   0-7424-1807-3 *Building Grammar & Writing Skills*

Table of Contents	Standards Reflected	Page
Part II: Writing Strategies		
Developing Writing Processes		
Identifying Topics		
Establishing Focus		
Developing Support		
Creating Structure		
Establishing Voice, Audience, and Purpose		

© McGraw-Hill Children's Publishing

0-7424-1807-3 *Building Grammar & Writing Skills*

0-7424-1807-3 *Building Grammar & Writing Skills*

Table of Contents	Standards Reflected	Page
Research Writing, continued		
Create a Works Cited Page	4, 5, 6	114
Put the Paper Together	4, 5, 6	115
Peer Review Form	4, 5, 6	116
Technical Documents		
General Guidelines	4, 5, 6, 11	117
Resumes	4, 5, 6, 8, 11, 12	118
Resume Cover Letter	4, 5, 6, 11, 12	119
Follow-Up Letter	4, 5, 6, 11, 12	120
Business Cards	4, 5, 6, 8, 11, 12	121
E-mail Messages	4, 5, 6, 8, 11, 12	122
Project Reports	4, 5, 6, 7, 8, 11	123
Write a Project Report	4, 5, 6, 7, 8, 11	124
Answer Key		125

© McGraw-Hill Children's Publishing

0-7424-1807-3 *Building Grammar & Writing Skills*

Name _____ Date _____

Capitals Rule!

Capital letters are tools writers use to tell a reader that a word is especially important for some reason. People sometimes omit capitalization altogether or they write in all capital letters for emphasis, especially when writing informal notes. However, many writing occasions require the use of Standard English, which has specific rules about when words should or should not be capitalized. Most of these rules help the writer to be clearer and more courteous. Failure to follow these rules can cause a reader to make negative judgments about a writer's ideas. When in doubt about whether to capitalize a word, check the dictionary.

Read the passage below. Study the capitalized words in bold type and try to identify five Standard English rules governing capitalization. Write your "rules" on the lines next to the appropriate numbers. The fourth rule is done for you.

Many [1] famous people have changed their names for one reason or another. **For** [1] example, **Mary Ann Evans** [2], one of **England's** [5] most famous novelists and author of many books, including *Silas Marner* [3], chose the pen name **George Eliot** [2] because she was writing in the **Victorian** [4] period, when most successful published writers were men. **She** [1] died in **London** [5], **England** [5], in 1880.

1. Capitalize _____

2. Capitalize _____

3. Capitalize _____

4. Capitalize historical periods.

5. Capitalize _____

Now check your rules against the list below. Put a check mark on the line beside those rules that you answered correctly. Underline the specific part of the rule reflected in the sentences above.

a. _____ Capitalize the names of days of the week, months, holidays, and historical periods.

b. _____ Capitalize the names of special events and geographical places.

c. _____ Capitalize the first word in a sentence and the first word in a quotation.

d. _____ Capitalize people's names, the titles of important people (when the title precedes the name), initials, and the pronoun *I*.

e. _____ Capitalize titles of works of art, books, newspapers, magazines, companies, and organizations.

9

Name _____ Date _____

Capital Etiquette

First Word in a Sentence and the First Word of a Quotation.
Capitalizing the first word in a sentence lets the reader know where a new idea begins.

> <u>One</u> of the all-time great American classics is *Huckleberry Finn*.

Sometimes a sentence is found inside another sentence, as when a person's words are quoted. In such cases, both sentence beginnings are capitalized.

> <u>Fans</u> of Clint Eastwood love it every time he says, "<u>Make</u> my day."

Names, Titles, Initials, and the Pronoun *I*. *Proper noun* is the term given to nouns that name specific people or things, and they are capitalized both as a matter of courtesy and as a way of telling the reader how to respond to the word. For example, the word *cat* is a common noun and is not capitalized. However, if a writer spoke of a specific cat named "Casey," the name would be capitalized. Similarly, people's names are always capitalized, as are their initials and titles when the title precedes the name. Also, the pronoun *I* is always capitalized.

> <u>Samuel Langhorne Clemens</u> is better known as <u>Mark Twain</u>.
>
> Although <u>Dr.</u> Bill Cosby has an advanced degree in education, he is better known as a television star.
>
> <u>R. L.</u> Stine is a writer who is popular with young readers.
>
> My friends and <u>I</u> love to read and go to movies.

Correct the sentences below by capitalizing (1) words that begin a sentence, (2) words that begin a quotation, and (3) names, titles, initials, and the pronoun *I*.

1. actress jennifer anniston was born jennifer anastassakis in Sherman Oaks, California, on February 11, 1969. she is best known for her role as rachel in the television show *Friends*.

2. andy garcia is probably best known for his role in *The Godfather III*, for which he earned an Oscar nomination. information i found said that he was born on April 12, 1956, in Havana, Cuba, with the name andres arturo garcia menendez.

3. one source says this about the famous actor, director, comedian, musician, and screenwriter woody allen: "born allen stewart konigsberg [his initials were a.s.k.], he attended New York University after high school, where he failed motion picture production."

4. star of romantic comedies and dramas, meg ryan began her career in the soap opera *As the World Turns*. it is easy to see why miss ryan shortened her name. she was born

10

Name _____ Date _____

Of Uppercase Importance

Capitalize the titles of each of the following:
  Works of art (movies, paintings, and musical compositions):
    Star Wars, Mona Lisa
  Publications (books, newspapers, articles, poems, essays):
    Charlotte's Web, *Peoria Journal Star*, "The Road Not Taken,"
    "Letter from a Birmingham Jail"
  Companies: McDonald's, New Line Cinema, McGraw-Hill Publishing
  Organizations: University of Illinois, Democratic Party, First Presbyterian Church

The following passage contains nine capitalization errors with at least one from each of the above rules. Find the errors and write the correct form of the word in the appropriate box below. Note: only nine of the twelve boxes will be filled.

One of Hollywood's biggest stars, Tom Cruise was born Thomas Cruise Mapother IV in Syracuse, New York, on July 3, 1962. He has starred in such money-makers as *top gun*, *born on the fourth of july*, and *mission impossible*. He has worked for numerous major studios, including universal, columbia tri-star, and paramount. Reviews of his movies can be seen in all major newspapers, such as the *chicago tribune* and the *new york times*. Cruise is a member of the church of scientology.

Works of Art	Publications	Companies	Organizations

Complete the following sentences, using appropriate capitalization:

  1. My favorite movie is _____

  2. My favorite book is _____

  3. My favorite restaurant is _____

11

Name _____ Date _____

We're Important Too!

Capitalize names of the days of the week, months of the year, holidays, and historical periods.

    Saturday   June   Groundhog Day   Middle Ages

Capitalize the names of special events and geographical places.

    Special Olympics   New York City   England

Revise the following sentences by crossing out inappropriate lowercase letters and replacing them with capital letters.

1. Known as "The Muscles from Brussels," Jean-Claude Van Damme was born Jean-Claude Van Varenberg in brussels, belgium, on october 18, 1960.

2. Born with the name Marion Michael Morrison in winterset, iowa, on may 26, 1907, John Wayne went on to become one of the world's best known movie stars. He was honored at the 1970 academy awards with an Oscar for his role in *True Grit*.

3. Whoopi Goldberg was born in new york on november 13, 1955, with the name of Caryn Elaine Johnson.

4. Write a sentence telling where and when you were born, capitalizing words as appropriate.

_____

_____

_____

5. Write a sentence that includes the name of your favorite holiday or your favorite sports event.

_____

_____

_____

6. Write a sentence that includes as many of the following as you can: day of the week, month, holiday, historical period, special event, and geographical place.

_____

_____

_____

_____

       0-7424-1807-3 *Building Grammar & Writing Skills*

Name _____ Date _____

Unconventional Capitalization

Media. Writers in the media often use capital letters in unusual ways to emphasize words or ideas. Do a little research on unconventional uses of capital letters in the world around you. Look at the Internet, newspaper articles, advertisements, labels on products, and signs or billboards to find five examples of unconventional uses of capital letters. In the spaces below, tell where you saw the word, what was being discussed or sold, what the word was, and how the capitalization deviated from Standard English.

Where did you find the word?	What was the article or ad discussing or selling?	What was the word?	What capitalization rule was broken?
Internet Newspaper Advertisement Product Label Sign or Billboard			

Poetry. Like advertisers, poets sometimes use capital letters in unconventional ways. Read the following stanza from Robert Service's poem, "The Heart of the Sourdough," about life in Alaska. What word in his poem is not normally capitalized in Standard English?

> With the raw-ribbed Wild that abhors all life,
> the Wild that would crush and rend,
> I have clinched and closed with the naked North,
> I have learned to defy and defend;
> Shoulder to shoulder we have fought it out—
> yet the Wild must win in the end.

Word _____ Why do you think Robert Service chose to capitalize this word?

_____

_____

_____

Name _____ Date _____

Capitalization Review

Pretend that you have become a famous person and have selected a pen name or stage name for yourself. You may want to follow the example of the famous people previously mentioned, who used some part of their original first or last name. Or, like John Wayne, you may want to choose a different name altogether. Write a short paragraph about your chosen name, telling why you selected it. Describe your imaginary career, including where you would go, what publications would write about you, and where and when your public appearances would occur. Or, if you prefer, write a press release in the role of a reporter from a magazine covering your appearance at some event. Try to use as many capital letters as you can from the five categories below. Underline each capitalized word and put the category number above the word.

Capitalization Categories

1. Capitalize the first word in a sentence and the first word in a quotation.
2. Capitalize people's names, the titles of important people, initials, and the pronoun *I*.
3. Capitalize titles of works of art, books, newspapers, magazines, companies, and organizations.
4. Capitalize the names of days of the week, months, holidays, and historical periods.
5. Capitalize the names of special events and geographical places.

Why I Would Choose to Be _____

_____

_____

_____

_____

_____

_____

_____

_____

_____

_____

_____

_____

_____

0-7424-1807-3 *Building Grammar & Writing Skills*

Name _____ Date _____

Punctuation Eliminates Confusion

Many of the punctuation errors that people make result from differences between the way people speak and the way they write. A speaker uses pauses and inflection (raising or lowering pitch, for example) to cue a listener on how to respond. Writers, on the other hand, need to provide written cues for their readers. Note that the following sentences could be read in three different ways—the end punctuation tells the reader how to respond.

Believe this.
Believe this?
Believe this!

Even punctuation in the middle of a sentence can be important to the reader's understanding. See whether you can figure out where a speaker would pause in the following sentence. Place a comma after the appropriate word.

As he walked the dog ran happily ahead of him.

You probably saw that a pause after the word *walked* helped you to make sense of the words.

Below is a passage from *Anne of Green Gables* with punctuation removed. See whether you can guess what punctuation the author, Lucy Maude Montgomery, used. If you guess correctly, you will use all of the marks of punctuation listed below (the number in parentheses tells how many of each she used). Capitalize words that you think should begin sentences. Discuss your choices with classmates before looking at Montgomery's choices.

Periods	(6)
Question marks	(3)
Exclamation marks	(1)
Quotation marks	(4)
Commas	(5)

Do you know said Anne confidentially i've made up my mind to enjoy this drive it's been my experience that you can nearly always enjoy things if you make up your mind firmly that you will of course you must make it up FIRMLY i am not going to think about going back to the asylum while we're having our drive i'm just going to think about the drive oh look there's one little early wild rose out isn't it lovely don't you think it must be glad to be a rose wouldn't it be nice if roses could talk i'm sure they could tell us such lovely things

Name _____ Date _____

End Marks

Punctuation marks that signal the end of a sentence are of three types: periods, question marks, and exclamation marks. Each type of mark creates a different response from the reader. A period follows a **declarative sentence,** which makes a statement or provides information to the reader without asking for a particular response.

Example: The mosquitoes are especially fierce this year.

A question mark follows an **interrogative sentence,** which asks a question. Readers are expected to respond with an answer, at least in their minds.

Example: Why do mosquitoes pick on some people and not others?

An exclamation mark follows an **exclamatory sentence,** which tells the reader to respond with surprise, delight, or other strong emotion. Most good writers use this mark of punctuation sparingly to avoid the appearance of overexaggeration.

Example: There, I got one!

Provide the best end punctuation for each of the following sentences.

   1. Do you believe that Mighty Mouse can really fly

   2. I believe that he can

   3. You must be crazy

   4. Write a declarative sentence, telling something complimentary about one of your friends.

   _____

   _____

   5. Write an interrogative sentence, asking a question about the outcome of a sports event.

   _____

   _____

   6. Write an exclamatory sentence about some frightening experience you have had.

   _____

   _____

   7. Write three sentences about your cooking abilities—one declarative sentence, one interrogative sentence, and one exclamatory sentence.

   _____

   _____

   _____

16

Name _____ Date _____

Comma: The In,ter,rupt,er

Commas are marks that tell a reader to make a short pause, rather than the longer pause suggested by a period. Comma errors that are most likely to offend readers are those that cause confusion. Sometimes the confusion results from using commas when they should not be used, and other times the confusion occurs because necessary commas have been omitted. Most commas are used to separate interrupters (nonessential comments and descriptive information) from the rest of the sentence.

Interrupters. Use commas to separate words and phrases that interrupt the sentence. Sentence interrupters can be as short as a single word, or they can be long phrases or clauses. To test whether a word or group of words is really an interrupter, imagine that you are picking the interrupting words right out of the sentence. The remaining words should still make sense. The interrupters in the following examples are in brackets.

Lake Superior, [the largest of the Great Lakes], produces abundant trout and whitefish.

The temperature, [however], is quite cold for swimmers.

Supply the necessary commas in the following sentences. Put interrupting material in brackets.

1. Ernie and Karel who love to fish for Muskies bought a new fishing boat to take to Lake of the Woods.

2. Their plans unfortunately had to be cancelled this year.

Introductory Words, Phrases, and Clauses. Use commas after introductory words, phrases, and clauses. Notice in the second example below that if the introductory information is moved to the end of the sentence, there is no comma.

Because they had to postpone the trip, the fishermen were very disappointed.

The fishermen were very disappointed because they had to postpone the trip.

Supply necessary commas in the following sentences.

3. However the fishermen intend to make it up to the lake next year.

4. At the first opportunity they will be on their way to the great waters of the North.

5. Rewrite sentence 4 to put the introductory information at the end of the sentence.

_____

_____

0-7424-1807-3 *Building Grammar & Writing Skills*

Name _____ Date _____

Commas Give Us Pause

Words, Phrases, and Clauses in a Series. Use a comma between items in a series of three or more words, phrases, or clauses. Failure to use necessary commas can confuse readers. The first sentence below is punctuated correctly. The second is not. See whether you can figure out where the commas go in the second sentence.

> My favorite water sports are swimming, water skiing, and canoeing.

> Juan searched under the boat on the shore and down the river after tipping over the canoe and losing his camera keys and wallet.

Without the commas in the second sentence, it looks as though the boat is on the shore and Juan has keys for his camera. You probably guessed that commas need to go after *boat, shore, camera,* and *keys.* Write a sentence describing at least three places you would look if you lost your keys, watch, or billfold. Use commas to separate the items in a series.

_____

_____

Commas in Dates and Locations. Use commas to separate days, months, and years. Notice that the comma between the day of the month and the year helps to keep the numbers from running together. Also, use commas to separate cities and states.

> Jenny was born on Thursday, January 16, 1986, in St. Joseph's Hospital.

> Nicole goes to college in Gainesville, Florida, where she is majoring in marketing.

Add the necessary commas in the following sentences.

1. The telethon next year will be held on Saturday March 22 2003 in Ottawa Illinois.

2. Uncle Bob was born on November 20 1938 in Toronto Ontario Canada.

Fill in the blanks in the following sentences.

3. I was born on _____ in _____
             (day/month/date/year)   (city/state)

4. Christmas this year falls on _____
                                  (day/month/date)

5. Write several original sentences about a favorite trip or vacation—one that you have taken or would like to take. Include dates, locations, and items in a series, demonstrating your knowledge of comma usage.

0-7424-1807-3 *Building Grammar & Writing Skills*

Name _____ Date _____

Cordial and Carried Away Commas

Use commas after the greeting of a friendly letter and after the closing in all letters.

	Friendly Letter	**Business Letter**
Greeting	Dear Leda,	Dear Ms. Burton:
Closing	Sincerely, Joe	Sincerely, Joe McLennan

Pretend that you are writing a letter to a friend. Fill in the blanks, adding commas where needed:

Dear _____

Sincerely

_____

Inappropriate Comma Use. Commas should not be used to separate independent clauses (groups of words that can stand alone as a sentence), which need a longer pause created by a semicolon or the addition of a coordinating conjunction (*and, or, but, nor, for, yet, so*).

Wrong: Mary loves to play golf, she built a putting green in her backyard.
Correct: Mary loves to play golf, so she built a putting green in her backyard.
Correct: Mary loves to play golf. She built a putting green in her backyard.
Correct: Mary loves to play golf; she built a putting green in her backyard.

Commas should not be used to separate subjects and verbs or verbs and objects.
Notice that the commas in the first two sentences below ask readers to pause inappropriately.

Wrong: Gary and Karla, hoped their friends could come to their party.
Wrong: Gary and Karla hoped, their friends could come to their party.
Correct: Gary and Karla hoped their friends could come to their party.

In the blank at the left of each sentence, write a *C* if the comma is used correctly.
Write a *W* if the comma is inappropriately placed.

____ **1.** Garret loves to play chess, and he's very good at it.

____ **2.** He sometimes pretends to know less than he does, he can trick his opponent that way.

____ **3.** Garrett's sudden checkmate comes, as a surprise to his opponent.

4. Write a sentence with two independent clauses joined by a comma and coordinating conjunction. _____

_____

19

 0-7424-1807-3 *Building Grammar & Writing Skills*

Name _____ Date _____

A Bigger Break: Semicolons and Colons

Semicolons. Semicolons alert the reader to a major pause in a sentence—a pause greater than that of a comma but less than a period. Use semicolons to join two main clauses when the ideas are closely related; when the clauses are joined by words like *however, consequently*, or *therefore*; and to separate items in a series when the items themselves include commas (as in this sentence).

Burnie is not just a horse; she's my friend.

Shetan can be a challenge; however, he knows lots of tricks.

Read the following passage, written by the English poet William Thackeray. Then, in the lines below, write a similar passage of your own, using semicolons to emphasize a humorous point. Write about some practice in your home or school.

King George's household was a model of an English gentleman's household. It was early; it was kindly; it was charitable; it was frugal; it was orderly; it must have been stupid to a degree that I shudder now to contemplate. No wonder all the princes ran away.

_____

_____

_____

_____

Colons. Colons are used to introduce lists that follow a main clause or to introduce a long quotation.
Example: I love all horses, but I have three favorites: Quarter horses, Arabians, and Paints.

Write a sentence identifying three of your favorite sports in a list that follows a colon.

_____

_____

Colons separate hours and minutes. They also follow the greeting of a formal letter.
My favorite class, art, begins at 10:20 A.M.   Dear Ms. Peters:

On the lines below, write the name and time of your favorite class and a formal greeting to the teacher.

_____   _____   Dear _____
(name of class)   (time it begins)   (name of the teacher)

                    0-7424-1807-3 *Building Grammar & Writing Skills*

Name _____ Date _____

"Who Said I Slant?" She Asked

Use quotation marks to enclose the exact words of a speaker:

"The time has come,"
the Walrus said,
"To talk of many things:
Of shoes and ships—and sealing wax—
Of cabbages—and kings—
And why the sea is boiling hot—
And whether pigs have wings."

Use quotation marks to enclose titles of short works, such as poems, stories, or songs. Use italics to indicate titles of long works, such as books, magazines, newspapers, plays, and movies.

The lines above are from a poem called "The Walrus and the Carpenter," from a chapter entitled "Tweedledum and Tweedledee," in Lewis Carroll's book *Through the Looking Glass*.

Find an article in a newspaper or magazine. Write a short review of the article, telling briefly what it says, whether you agree, and why. Use at least one direct quotation (exact words of the writer) from the article. Begin your review by telling where you got your information. Underline the title of the magazine or newspaper (when writing by hand, it is customary to underline words that should be italicized). Put the title of the article in quotation marks.

_____

_____

_____

_____

_____

_____

_____

_____

_____

_____

Name _____ Date _____

Punctuation Review

Find an advertisement on TV, on a billboard, or in newspapers or magazines using at least five types of punctuation. Choose from the following list:

Periods   Semicolons   Italics

Question marks   Colons   Commas

Exclamation marks   Quotation marks

Write the advertisement here, and circle the punctuation marks.

_____

_____

_____

_____

_____

_____

_____

_____

Write an original advertisement for a new type of tennis shoe.
Use at least five types of punctuation from the list above. Circle the punctuation marks.

_____

_____

_____

_____

_____

_____

_____

_____

22

Name _____ Date _____

He Agrees That We Agree

In Standard English, a verb always agrees with its subject. If the subject is singular (dog, mouse), the verb is singular and ends with an –s (dog *is*, mouse *scurries*). If the subject is plural (dogs, mice), the verb is plural and does not end with an –s (dogs *are*, mice *scurry*).

When a prepositional phrase appears between the subject and the verb, the verb must agree with the subject and not the object of the preposition. An easy way to focus on the subject is to read the sentence without the interrupting prepositional phrase.
Example with phrase: The writer *with three published stories* reads mysteries. When read without the prepositional phrase, the subject and verb appear side by side: The <u>writer</u> *reads* mysteries.

When a sentence contains two subjects joined with *and*, the verb is plural and, therefore, does not end with an –s.
   The novel and the article *reveal* accurate information.
   The novel and the articles *contain* current information.
   The novels and the articles *are* interesting.

If two subject are joined by *or* or *nor*, the subject closer to the verb is used to determine agreement.
   The novels or the <u>article</u> *is* on the desk.
   The novel or the <u>articles</u> *are* helpful.

Finish each sentence using correct subject–verb agreement. Use present tense verbs.

   1. St. Louis and Kansas City _____

   2. The editor with his three assistants _____

   3. The girls and their brother _____

   4. Either Jason or the twins _____

   5. Golf or bowling _____

   6. Neither the houses nor the apartment building _____

   7. The athletes on the team _____

   8. A poem, a fable, and an essay _____

   9. Two cantaloupe or one watermelon _____

   10. Several novels and poems _____

Name _____ Date _____

Everybody Agrees, But Few Concur

When pronouns replace nouns as subjects of sentences, they also must agree in number with the verb of the sentence.

Some indefinite pronouns are always singular and, therefore, always take verbs that end with an −s. Singular indefinite pronouns include *anyone, anybody, anything, everyone, everybody, everything, someone, somebody, something, no one, nobody, nothing, each, either, neither,* and *every*.

Other indefinite pronouns are always plural; verbs that follow them are plural and do not end with an −s. Plural indefinite pronouns are *both, few, many, others,* and *several*.

Yet other indefinite pronouns can be either singular or plural depending upon how they are used in the sentence. Those are *all, any, most, much, none,* and *some*. If the indefinite pronoun refers to a quantity, the verb is singular and ends with an −s. (All of the <u>mail</u> *was* late yesterday.) If the indefinite pronoun refers to items that can be counted, the verb is plural and does not end with an −s. (All of the <u>letters</u> *were mailed* last week.)

Finish the following sentence beginnings with verbs that show correct agreement. Use present tense verbs or linking verbs *was* and *were*.

1. Both _____

2. Everyone _____.

3. Some of the milk _____.

4. Some of the glasses _____

5. Many of the assignments _____

6. None of the sand _____.

7. Few of her errors _____.

8. No one _____.

9. None of David's story _____.

10. None of David's sentences _____.

Write two original sentences using correct subject–verb agreement. In the first include a singular indefinite pronoun, and in the second include a plural indefinite pronoun.

1. _____

2. _____

24

0-7424-1807-3 *Building Grammar & Writing Skills*

Name _____ Date _____

Adjectives and Adverbs Add Detail

Since adjectives and adverbs modify other parts of speech, they enhance sentences with details. Yet when too many adjectives or adverbs appear in a series, each one loses its impact. To avoid overwhelming their readers, experienced writers refrain from adding more modifiers and instead concentrate on using strong verbs and on using only the best modifiers to make their writing more powerful.

Original:	The large, crisp, juicy apple satisfied Danielle's hunger.
Revised:	The apple, crisp and juicy, satisfied Danielle's hunger.
Original:	Jimmy glided quickly, effortlessly, and confidently across the ice.
Revised:	Quickly and effortlessly, Jimmy glided across the ice.
Revised:	Jimmy glided across the ice quickly and effortlessly.

Create sentences that follow the patterns below. The first one has been done as an example. Delete modifiers that do not enhance the description.

1. adjective–conjunction–adjective (at beginning of sentence)
   I won't make that mistake again because I'm older; I am also wiser.
   Older and wiser, I won't make that mistake again!

2. adverb–conjunction–adverb (at end of sentence)
   Tara answered the question quickly. Tara answered the question decisively.

   _____

3. adverb–conjunction–adverb (at beginning of sentence)
   Samantha reread her essay carefully, slowly.

   _____

4. The–adjective–adjective–noun (at beginning of sentence)
   The tall man lumbered down the street.
   The dark man lumbered down the street with his cloak flowing.

   _____

5. The–noun–adjective–conjunction–adjective (at beginning of sentence)
   The visitor was flamboyant; the visitor was daring.
   The visitor walked down the street at midnight.

   _____

Create two sentences of your own, using the patterns below somewhere in your sentences.

adjective–conjunction–adjective _____

adverb–conjunction–adverb _____

0-7424-1807-3 *Building Grammar & Writing Skills*

Name _____ Date _____

Verb Phrases

A verb phrase consists of the main verb and one or more helping verbs. Verb phrases can consist of two, three, or four words: *do walk, have been walking,* and *could have been running.* A writer's choice of verb tense depends upon the writing task. Writers usually choose past tense when they discuss events that have already happened, present tense when they write reviews and summaries or when they explain events occurring in the present, and future tense when they wish to discuss events that have not yet occurred. Writers may also choose progressive forms to show continuing action and emphatic forms to emphasize action. The following chart depicts three forms of verbs commonly used.

	Basic	**Progressive**	**Emphatic**
Present	write	am/is/are writing	do/does write
Past	wrote	was writing	did write
Future	will write	will be writing	
Present Perfect	have/has written		
Past Perfect	had written		
Future Perfect	will have written		

Use the correct verb phrase to designate the tense in the following sentences.

1. [work–past progressive] Jack London _____ on the short story "To Build a Fire" while on a boat in the South Seas.

2. [write–past perfect] He actually _____ a shorter version of "To Build a Fire" six years before he rewrote it.

3. [live–past perfect] He _____ in the Klondike where he searched for gold.

4. [read–future] Our class _____ both versions of his famous tale.

5. [write–present emphatic] We all agree that London _____ an exciting adventure.

6. [write–present progressive] Our class _____reviews of his novel *White Fang.*

7. [revise–future progressive] I _____ the reviews.

8. [edit–future] Jeremy _____ the essays before they are published.

Listen to conversations in the hallway, in the cafeteria, or at home. From those conversations, create three original sentences using the verb forms below.

1. Past Perfect Basic _____.

2. Future Progressive _____.

3. Present Emphatic _____.

0-7424-1807-3 *Building Grammar & Writing Skills*

Name _____ Date _____

Infinitive Phrases

An infinitive phrase contains an infinitive (to + a verb) and modifiers or other words that complete its meaning.

>   to run quickly (infinitive plus a modifier)
>   to run a good race (infinitive plus a direct object)

Because they can function as nouns (subjects, direct objects, and predicate nouns), adjectives, and adverbs, infinitives give writers many options.

>   *To read five novels a month* is Christine's goal. (noun–subject)
>   Christine's goal is *to read five novels a month*. (noun–predicate noun)
>   Christine's sister refused *to read even four novels*. (noun–direct object)
>   A good poem *to read* is "The Bells" by Edgar Allan Poe. (adjective)
>   Joan purchases newspapers *to read book and movie reviews*. (adverb)

Note: Infinitive phrases should not be confused with prepositional phrases beginning with *to*. He drove <u>to the store</u> (prepositional phrase) *to purchase a gallon of ice cream*.

Using the following sentences as models, create original sentences with infinitive phrases.

1. infinitive phrase used as a subject—To observe details is a trait of a good writer.

    _____

2. infinitive phrase used as a direct object—Sarah wanted to become a sports writer since she started watching basketball on television.

    _____

3. infinitive phrase used as an adjective—The best essays to write with detail and emotion are those that stem from personal experiences.

    _____

4. infinitive phrase used as a predicate noun—Matthew's favorite pastime last summer was to ride his horse.

    _____

5. infinitive phrase used as an adverb—Jordan found it easy to proofread his final drafts on the computer screen.

    _____

27

0-7424-1807-3 *Building Grammar & Writing Skills*

Name _____ Date _____

Participial Phrases

A participle is a verb form that functions as an adjective. There are two types of participles: present participles and past participles. Present participles always end with *-ing*. Past participles usually end with *–d* or *–ed* unless they are formed from irregular verbs. Participial phrases consist of a participle and modifying words and phrases.

Participles Created from Regular Verbs

Present Participle: *tiring* jobs   Past Participle: *tired* travelers

Present Participial Phrase: *Stumbling along the path*, Jared reached for a branch.

Past Participial Phrase: *Frustrated about his piano lesson*, Cody practiced reluctantly.

Participles Created from Irregular Verbs

Present Participle: *breaking* glass   Past Participle: *broken* glass

Present Participial Phrase: *Bursting with color*, the flower garden attracted butterflies.

Past Participial Phrase: The paper, *torn to shreds*, lay on the bottom of the wastebasket.

Participial phrases often make sentences more vivid by blending action with description.

Create vivid sentences by adding a participial phrase immediately before or after the noun it modifies. If a participial phrase begins a sentence, a comma follows it. The first one is done for you.

1. The storm unleashed its fury.

Pelting the city with sleet, the storm unleashed its fury.

2. Jayne blamed her brother.

_____

3. The man avoided the St. Bernard.

_____

4. The child laughed at the clown's antics.

_____

5. Samantha crossed the finish line first.

_____

6. Our town is a great place to live.

_____

28

Name _____ Date _____

Independent Clauses

All clauses contain subjects and verbs. Independent clauses not only contain subjects and verbs, but they also make sense as sentences. A simple sentence contains one independent clause. A compound sentence contains two (or more) independent clauses.

Compound sentences are usually connected with a comma and a coordinating conjunction: *and, but, or, for, so,* and *yet.* Sometimes a semicolon connects the clauses; in this case a coordinating conjunction does not follow the semicolon.

Simple Sentence:	Jason read a newspaper article about Lance Armstrong.
Compound Sentence:	Armstrong battled cancer, but he overcame the disease to win the Tour de France.
Compound Sentence:	The Tour de France is a bicycle race; it includes over twenty stages.

Rewrite the following sentence fragments into complete sentences. You may create either simple or compound sentences, but be certain to punctuate them correctly. After you have written the sentence, label it *S* for simple and *C* for compound on the short line provided.

1. ____ currently thirty major league baseball stadiums.

2. ____ Fenway Park in Boston, Massachusetts, being the oldest Wrigley Field in Chicago, Illinois, the second oldest

3. ____ Qualcomm Stadium in San Diego, California, largest capacity—over 65,000 fans

4. ____ once called Jack Murphy Stadium now called Qualcomm Stadium

5. ____ Three new parks having opened 2000: Minute Maid, Comerica, and Pacific Bell

6. ____ Play having begun on April 6, 2001, at PNC Park, and play having begun on April 9, 2001, at Miller Park

7. ____ Have seen Olympic Stadium in Montreal? Sky Dome in Toronto?

29

  0-7424-1807-3 *Building Grammar & Writing Skills*

Name _____ Date _____

Dependent Clauses: Adjective

Like an independent clause, a dependent clause (also called a subordinate clause) contains a subject and a verb. However, unlike an independent clause, a dependent clause cannot stand alone as a sentence. Because a dependent clause cannot stand alone, it is combined with an independent clause to create a complex sentence.

One type of dependent clause is the adjective clause. Adjective clauses always begin with relative pronouns: *who, whose, whom, which,* and *that.* Like adjectives, they modify nouns and pronouns.

Use a relative pronoun to combine the sentences below. Be certain to begin each dependent clause with *who, whose, whom, which,* or *that.* Write the combined sentence on the lines.

1. [who] Samuel Langhorne Clemens is better known as Mark Twain. Clemens lived in Hannibal, Missouri, from 1839 to 1853.

_____

2. [that] Many characters in *The Adventures of Tom Sawyer* are based upon people. Twain knew these people when he lived in Hannibal.

_____

3. [whose] Among characters based on people is Tom. Tom's character was created from characteristics of two friends and from parts of Twain himself.

_____

4. [who] Mark Twain created another memorable character, Becky Thatcher. Becky was based on a family neighbor.

_____

5. [which] The cave appears in the novel. The cave is most likely based on McDowell's Cave in Hannibal, Missouri.

_____

6. [that] Mark Twain may have included the cave in his book after he read a newspaper article. The article appeared in the *St. Louis Democrat* in the spring of 1874.

_____

7. [whom] William Dean Howells was a fellow author and a friend of Twain. Twain received advice from Howells concerning the novel.

_____

30

Name _____ Date _____

Dependent Clauses: Adverb

Another type of dependent clause is the adverb clause. Adverb clauses begin with subordinating conjunctions. Commonly used subordinating conjunctions include the following:

after	although	as	because	before
if	since	unless	until	when

A subject and a verb will follow subordinating conjunctions that begin dependent clauses. Unlike the relative pronouns, *who, which,* and *that,* subordinating conjunctions cannot function as subjects of dependent clauses.

Create complex sentences with dependent clauses by combining the following simple sentences. Choose a subordinating conjunction from the above list.

1. Many strategies exist to help students. Students often have problems with the writing proceses.

   _____

2. The assignment or deadline is not due soon. Writers may put the draft away for a period of time.

   _____

3. Many professional writers write much more than they use. They find it easier to delete unimportant "extra" information rather than to think of new material.

   _____

   _____

4. They submit their work to publishers. Many professional writers ask trusted friends to read their drafts and give advice.

   _____

   _____

5. Writing every day seems rigorous. Nearly every professional author follows a daily writing routine.

   _____

6. Beginning writers will likely find the above strategies beneficial. They experience difficulty finishing a writing assignment.

   _____

   _____

31

Name _____ Date _____

Usage Review

Listen to and read various media to find sentences that reflect what you learned in this section. Write the sentence on the line provided and indicate the media source from which you obtained the sentence.

1. Sentence with vivid adjectives (Source _____)

_____

2. Sentence with vivid adverbs (Source _____)

_____

3. Sentence containing an infinitive phrase (Source _____)

_____

4. Sentence containing a participial phrase (Source _____)

_____

5. A compound sentence (Source _____)

_____

_____

6. A complex sentence with an adjectival dependent clause (Source _____)

_____

_____

7. A complex sentence with an adverbial dependent clause (Source _____)

_____

_____

Which types of sentences were easiest to find? _____

Circle the media sources that provided the most variety.

Newspapers   Magazines   Web Sites

Radio   Television   Billboards

Other (explain) _____

_____

0-7424-1807-3 *Building Grammar & Writing Skills*

Name _____ Date _____

Know Your Nouns

Parts of speech are grammatical categories, with names for words that give readers and writers common labels for discussion purposes. These terms are especially useful when readers and writers wish to describe the function of words in a sentence. The noun, one of eight parts of speech, establishes what a sentence is about and, therefore, is a good place to begin.

A noun is the name of a person, place, thing, or idea.
Label the following nouns: person, place, thing, or idea.

_____	1. desk	_____	6. cloud
_____	2. sister-in-law	_____	7. park
_____	3. friend	_____	8. Tiger Woods
_____	4. San Francisco	_____	9. writer
_____	5. happiness	_____	10. computer

Circle the words in the sentences below that are nouns.

1. Penguins are seabirds that can walk upright just like humans.

2. Their legs are short, causing them to waddle.

3. Scientists have noted that penguins can swim much faster than humans.

4. Their short, compact feathers and thick layer of fat insulate them against the cold.

5. Penguins can be found in New Zealand, Australia, and South Africa.

6. Because of their curiosity, penguins are considered social creatures.

7. Although penguins swim much of the time, they lay their eggs on land.

8. After the female penguin lays an egg, the male keeps it warm.

9. If you would like to study penguins, you may see them at a zoo.

10. They also can be found in Antarctica.

33

Name _____ Date _____

Types of Nouns

Types of nouns include

1. Common noun: a general person, place, thing, or idea (boy, house)

2. Proper noun: a specific person, place, thing, or idea; it is capitalized
(Frank Lloyd Wright, Phoenix, Arizona, Democracy)

3. Concrete noun: a noun that has substance and can be seen or touched (desk, tree)

4. Abstract noun: names an idea; it does not have substance and cannot be seen or touched
(honesty, courage, friendship)

5. Collective noun: names groups (flock, band, audience)

6. Compound noun: noun consisting of separate words (Empire State Building),
hyphenated words (self-esteem), or two words written as one (playground)

Notice that some nouns may fall into more than one of the above categories. For example, in the
sentence <u>Janice enjoys playing *volleyball*</u>, the word *volleyball* is common, concrete, and compound.

Label how each italicized noun is used in the following sentences.

1. Many sources provide *writers* (a) with *inspiration* (b) for their stories.
a. _____ b. _____

2. One of those sources, personal experiences, gave both *Jack London* (a)
and Mark Twain material for their short *stories* (b) and novels.
a. _____ b. _____

3. Even today Twain continues to delight his *audience* (a) of readers with anecdotes
of Tom Sawyer, which were based on his *boyhood* (b) in Hannibal, Missouri.
a. _____ b. _____

4. Jack London traveled to the *Yukon* (a) and searched for *gold* (b).
a. _____ b. _____

5. London's *success* (a) resulted from the *experiences* (b) he brought home rather
than the amount of gold he found.
a. _____ b. _____

6. London used these experiences in the novel *The Call of the Wild* (a),
a book about a dog that eventually runs with a *pack* (b) of wolves.
a. _____ b. _____

Think of a place, either near or far, where you have traveled. In one or more paragraphs,
describe this place. In a final paragraph, discuss ways you could use this place as source
material for your own writing. Write your response on another sheet of paper. Then list the
nouns you included in your writing and label the type of each noun.

34

Name _____ Date _____

Functions of Nouns

Nouns function as subjects, direct objects, predicate nouns, objects of prepositions, indirect objects, appositives, and nouns of direct address. Notice how they are used in the following sentences.

> Many *sources* [subject] give *writers* [indirect object] *ideas* [direct object] for their *stories* [object of preposition].
>
> One of those sources, a writer's personal *experiences* [appositive], is an excellent *place* [predicate noun] to begin brainstorming.
>
> *Writers* [noun of direct address], get ready to examine events from your past.

Using the number in front of each function, label how each italicized noun is used in the sentences below.

(1) subject	(2) direct object	(3) predicate noun	(4) object of preposition
(5) indirect object	(6) appositive	(7) noun of direct address	

1. *Students* ____, begin your *session* ____ by thinking of childhood *memories* ____.

2. Many *writers* ____ recall childhood *events* ____ complete with emotional *reactions* ____.

3. Others remember the *places* ____ they traveled for settings, language *patterns*, ____ and *characters* ____.

4. Another rich category is *employment* ____, the odd *jobs* ____ writers held before becoming well-known authors.

5. For example, *Mark Twain* ____ was a riverboat *pilot* ____ , and Jack London worked at both a jute *mill* ____ and a bowling alley.

6. Dreams, both daydreams and nighttime *dreams* ____, offer *writers* _____ yet another *category* ___ to examine.

7. Mary Shelley based her novel *Frankenstein* ____ on a *nightmare* ____ she had.

8. Use the next few *minutes* ____, *students* ____, to think about your personal *experiences* ____.

In one or two paragraphs, write about a personal experience. Like the writers in the above sentences, your experience may reveal a childhood event, travel memories, an odd job, or a dream. On another sheet of paper list all nouns you have used and their functions.

 0-7424-1807-3 Building Grammar & Writing Skills

Name _____ Date _____

Become Pronoun Pros

Pronouns are valuable tools in a writer's repertoire because they allow writers to avoid repeating the same noun throughout the text.

Personal Pronouns. The following chart shows the most frequently used pronouns, personal pronouns. You will notice three headings—subjective, (sometimes called nominative), possessive, and objective—at the top of the chart. These words denote how the pronouns are used in sentences and are called cases. The subjective case designates pronouns used as subjects and predicate nouns (nominatives). The objective case refers to pronouns used as direct objects, indirect objects, and objects of prepositions. The possessive case shows ownership.

	Subjective	Possessive	Objective
1st person, singular	I	my, mine	me
2nd person, singular	you	your, yours	you
3rd person, singular	he, she, it	his, her, hers, its	him, her, it
1st person, plural	we	our, ours	us
2nd person, plural	you	your, yours	you
3rd person, plural	they	their, theirs	them

From the above personal pronoun chart, select the appropriate pronoun and use it in an original sentence.

1. third person, singular–subjective, masculine _____

_____

2. first person, plural–possessive _____

_____

3. second person, singular and plural–objective _____

_____

4. first person, singular–objective _____

_____

5. third person, singular–objective, masculine _____

_____

6. second person, plural–possessive _____

_____

7. first person, plural–objective _____

_____

8. third person, singular–possessive, feminine _____

_____

0-7424-1807-3 Building Grammar & Writing Skills

Name _____ Date _____

Who Knows These Pronouns?

Demonstrative Pronouns. Demonstrative pronouns point out either someone or something. There are only four demonstrative pronouns: *this, that, these,* and *those.* As the following examples show, *this* and *that* are singular; *these* and *those* are plural. *This* and *these* refer to items close by, and *that* and *those* refer to items at a distance.

> The proofreader enjoyed reading *those* books.
> *This* manuscript contains several original similes.

Reflexive and Intensive Pronouns. Reflexive and intensive pronouns end with *–self* when they are singular and *–selves* when they are plural (*hisself* and *theirselves* are not words and, therefore, should not be used): *myself, yourself, himself, herself, itself, ourselves, yourselves,* and *themselves.* These pronouns are reflexive when they refer back to a noun; in this instance they usually follow a verb. They are intensive when they emphasize the noun before them; in this instance, they often appear immediately after the noun they emphasize. The following sentences demonstrate *himself* as both a reflexive and an intensive pronoun.

> Carlos gave *himself* ample time to revise his poem.   [reflexive]
> Ricardo *himself* will type the table of contents.   [intensive]

Interrogative Pronouns. Interrogative pronouns ask questions. They include *who, whose, whom, which,* and *what.* Notice how they are used in the following sentences.

> *Who* volunteered to format the class anthology of poetry?
> *Which* is the best way to begin the collection?

Complete each of the following sentences with a demonstrative, reflexive, intensive, or interrogative pronoun. Some sentences indicate a specific type of pronoun.

1. _____ [interrogative] would be a good title for the poetry anthology?

2. Louise said that she would draw the artwork _____ [reflexive].

3. The students _____ [intensive] decided to compile the anthology.

4. _____ [demonstrative] was a huge undertaking!

5. Pointing to the manuscript, Maria said, "Please give me _____."

6. "_____ are stanzas consisting of two lines each called?" Jon asked.

7. Nathan sold six anthologies _____.

8. Awards were given to the writers _____.

9. _____ wrote the longest poem?

10. _____ are fine poems.

37

Name _____ Date _____

Verbs: Regular and Irregular

Verbs express action or existence in sentences and, depending on the form, they also show tense. The principal parts of verbs along with auxiliary (also known as helping) verbs form verb tenses. Principal parts include present tense (infinitive), past tense, and past participle. The endings −d and −ed are added to regular verbs to create the past and past participle, while irregular verbs are formed in a variety of ways.

Fill in the correct principal parts of the verbs in the blank cells in each row of the chart below. Refer to a dictionary for the correct spelling of irregular verbs.

Present	Past	Past Participle
		has deleted
	revised	
finish		
create		
	saw	
		have written
	went	
bring		
		has burst
	made	

You probably noticed that the past participles contain helping (auxiliary) verbs. Auxiliary verbs help establish verb tense. Some (am, are, is, has, have, had) have meaning when used alone; others (can, may, might, must, could, should, would) are almost always used as auxiliary verbs.

Select a verb from the above chart. Write three original sentences using the correct form of the verb.

   1. Present

   _____

   _____

   2. Past

   _____

   _____

   3. Past Participle

   _____

   _____

38

Name _____ Date _____

No Stress Verb Tenses

From the principal parts of verbs you can form the six basic verb tenses listed below.
The first word in each pair is a regular verb (past tense formed by adding −*d* or −*ed*);
the second is an irregular verb.

Present: *work, think*   Present Perfect: *have worked, have thought*

Past: *worked, thought*   Past Perfect: *had worked, had thought*

Future: *will work, will think*   Future Perfect: *will have worked, will have thought*

Note that only the present and past tenses consist of one word; the others consist of one or more
auxiliary verbs plus the main verb. The auxiliary verb and the main verb together create a verb
phrase. Verb phrases also form the six progressive tenses:

     Present Progressive: *is working, is thinking*

     Past Progressive: *was working, was thinking*

     Future Progressive: *will be working, will be thinking*

     Present Perfect Progressive: *has been working, has been thinking*

     Past Perfect Progressive: *had been working, had been thinking*

     Future Perfect Progressive: *will have been working, will have been thinking*

Choose one regular verb and one irregular verb and write each tense.

Present _____   Present Perfect _____

Past _____   Past Perfect _____

Future _____   Future Perfect _____

Present Progressive _____   Present Perfect Progressive _____

Past Progressive _____   Past Perfect Progressive _____

Future Progressive _____   Future Perfect Progressive _____

Present _____   Present Perfect _____

Past _____   Past Perfect _____

Future _____   Future Perfect _____

Present Progressive _____   Present Perfect Progressive _____

Past Progressive _____   Past Perfect Progressive _____

Future Progressive _____   Future Perfect Progressive _____

On another sheet of paper write an original sentence for each of the verb tenses. You will have
24 sentences when you are through.

39

Name _____ Date _____

Adjectives Describe or Limit

Adjectives modify nouns or pronouns by describing or limiting them. Descriptive adjectives answer the question *what kind*, and limiting adjectives answer the questions *which one* and *how many*. Often descriptive adjectives appear before the noun they modify (*vivid* description), but they may also appear immediately after the noun they modify (the night, *dark* and *windy*) or after a linking verb. The following are types of adjectives, with their usual function in brackets.

1. article [limiting] *a, an, the*   Joe read *an* article in *the* magazine.

2. demonstrative [limiting] *this, that, these, those*   *This* article was short.

3. possessive nouns and pronouns [limiting] *his, her, its, my, our, your, their, Mia's*

                                                           Kendall lost *his* book.

4. interrogative [limiting] *which, what, whose*   *Which* magazine is your favorite?

5. numeric [limiting] *one, two, first, second*   Jason saw *two* movies.

6. predicate [descriptive] follow linking verbs *am, are, is, was, were*   Jo was *tired*.

7. proper [descriptive]   *Canadian* geese flew overhead.

Two types of verbs, the infinitive and the participial, also function as adjectives:

8. infinitive: to + verb   Jacob wanted a good video *to watch*.

9. participle: present—He liked the *exciting* chapters.   past—Hand in *edited* drafts only.

On the lines following each adjective, write the number of the type of adjective that appears in the sentence. Label descriptive adjectives *10* when they are not predicate or proper adjectives.

  1. In the 1831 _____ edition of *Frankenstein*, a _____ letter written by Mary Shelley outlines her _____ prewriting experience.

  2. Shelley's prewriting _____ experiences include sharing childhood stories with friends and walks in the dreary English _____ countryside.

  3. Shelley read ghost stories with her friends and had a wager with three _____ friends to write the best _____ ghost story.

  4. At that _____ time she experienced the inability to invent, which was miserable _____ for her.

  5. Finally she sketched a terrifying _____ nightmare, which became the most apparent _____ source for her _____ tale.

  6. Which _____ friend won the wager?

  7. Regardless who won, *Frankenstein* is a great _____ novel to read _____.

         0-7424-1807-3 Building Grammar & Writing Skills

Name _____ Date _____

Adverbs Anywhere and Everywhere

Adverbs modify verbs, adjectives, and other adverbs. Occasionally, they even modify entire clauses. Because adverbs modify several parts of speech, they may appear almost anywhere in a sentence and are more difficult to recognize than other parts of speech. The most common characteristic is the *–ly* ending of many adverbs. In addition to the *–ly* suffix, adverbs answer the questions *how, when, where, why,* and *to what extent* about the words they modify.

Some adverbs do not end in *–ly*: *very* quiet, *too* long, *quite* difficult, and others. Such adverbs usually answer the question, *to what extent*? Several adverbs, *here, there, where,* designate place.

Identify the adverbs in the sentences below by circling each one. Above each adverb write the letter of the questions the adverb answers.

A. How?   B. When?   C. Where?   D. Why?   E. To what extent?

1. Students of all ages intently read stories from Greek Mythology.

2. Even now readers enjoy learning about gods and goddesses.

3. Some myths explain natural phenomenon—why the seasons change and how spiders

    came to be.

4. Some myths show humans being rewarded for very good deeds or punished for misdeeds.

5. Baucis and Philemon were rewarded for being extremely kind; King Midas was punished

    for being too greedy.

6. Other myths tell tales of unusually brave heroes who travel far.

7. One hero, Theseus, finally got to Crete; there he bravely fought the Minotaur.

8. The Minotaur seemed to be everywhere; then it roared loudly.

9. Theseus soundly defeated the monster.

10. Nowadays readers soon understand that the Greeks created their stories without scientific

    knowledge to explain their existence.

0-7424-1807-3 Building Grammar & Writing Skills

Name _____ Date _____

Prepositions Like Company

Prepositions never appear by themselves in a sentence. They appear as the first word of a prepositional phrase and are followed by a noun or pronoun, which we call the *object* of the preposition. Prepositional phrases add detail to sentences by modifying nouns or pronouns when they function as adjectival phrases, and by modifying verbs, adjectives, or adverbs when they function as adverbial phrases. The most common prepositions follow.

about	around	besides	in	on	to
above	at	between	inside	out	under
across	before	by	into	over	until
after	behind	down	like	past	up
against	below	during	near	upon	with
along	beneath	for	of	since	within
among	beside	from	off	through	without

Study the prepositional phrases in the following sentences:

    The service *at the elegant restaurant* was incredibly fast.

In this sentence *at* is the preposition, *restaurant* is the object of the preposition, and *service* is the noun the prepositional phrase modifies. It is an adjectival prepositional phrase.

    Carmen placed her writing supplies *in the desk drawer*.

In the above sentence *in* is the preposition, *drawer* is the object of the preposition, and *placed* is the verb the prepositional phrase modifies. It is an adverbial prepositional phrase.

    Jeremy was born *in 1987*.

Numerals can be objects of prepositions; in the above sentence, *in* is the preposition and *1987* is the object of the preposition. The phrase modifies *was born*, making it an adverbial prepositional phrase.

In the following sentences, place parentheses around each prepositional phrase and underline the preposition. Above each phrase write *ADJ* if the phrase is used as an adjective and *ADV* if it is used as an adverb. Some sentences may contain more than one phrase.

1. Brandon read about paper currency.

2. Congress created the Federal Reserve System in 1913.

3. Under federal law, the Department of the Treasury and the Federal Reserve System issue currency in many denominations.

4. Cotton and linen rag paper with red and blue fibers is now used for paper currency.

5. Serial numbers with many digits are printed on all paper money.

6. The one-dollar bill has an average life span of 18 months.

7. Silver dollars were coined from 1794 to 1935.

0-7424-1807-3 Building Grammar & Writing Skills

Name _____ Date _____

Conjunctions and Interjections, Oh My!

Conjunctions serve to connect items in sentences, giving writers options to create sentence variety. With conjunctions writers create compound sentence parts, compound sentences, and complex sentences. Interjections allow writers to add emotion to their work and often give the writer a unique voice.

Coordinating Conjunctions. Coordinating conjunctions connect items of equal value. When used correctly, they connect two or more words, phrases, or clauses. Common coordinating conjunctions are *and, or, but, so, yet, for,* and *nor.*

Subordinating Conjunctions. Subordinating conjunctions connect items of unequal value. They usually connect a dependent (subordinate) clause to an independent clause. The dependent clauses begin with subordinating conjunctions and function as adverbs in the sentence. Frequently used subordinating conjunctions are *after, although, as, because, before, if, since, unless, until,* and *when.*

Correlative Conjunctions. Correlative conjunctions always appear in pairs. They include *either or, neither nor, both and,* and *not only...but also.*

Interjections. Interjections are words inserted in a sentence to emphasize a feeling; they have no grammatical function in regard to the structure of the sentence. Rather, they are words writers insert (or interject) into sentences to show strong emotion. Occasionally interjections improve a sentence, but to be effective they should be used sparingly. Notice how an exclamation mark follows the interjection in this example: Great! We are happy that you will be visiting us. Occasionally the interjection does not show strong feeling and is followed by a comma as in this example: Well, he will stay for one week.

In each sentence below fill in the blank with the conjunction that best completes the meaning of the sentence. Circle the interjection.

1. _____ Kevin _____ Kyle will forget the poem "The Highwayman."

2. The ballad tells a simple love story, _____ it also contains figures of speech.

3. Wow! The poem begins with _____ similes _____ metaphors.

4. In the poem the highwayman promises to return to Bess the next day with gold, _____

   Tim overhears the highwayman talking to Bess.

5. _____ Tim also loves Bess, he tells the Redcoats the highwayman's plans.

6. The ending reveals that _____ Tim _____ the highwayman marry Bess.

7. Kevin _____ Kyle were surprised that Bess sacrificed her life to save the highwayman.

43

Name _____ Date _____

Parts of Speech Review

After examining and working with the various parts of speech, you probably noticed that nouns and verbs make up the foundation of a sentence. Adjectives and adverbs add descriptive detail, and prepositions and conjunctions function as connecting elements. Pronouns replace nouns, and interjections add emphasis without affecting the structure of the sentence. You may also have noticed that a word may function as different parts of speech depending upon its use in a sentence.

> We have much *work* to complete before the end of the day. [noun]
> We *work* very hard every day. [verb]
> Most of my friends have a good *work* ethic. [adjective]

Review the parts of speech while writing a poem about yourself. Begin each line with a different part of speech. Although you may arrange the parts of speech in any order, you must include all eight parts of speech. Give your poem a title. Write your first draft below, labeling the part of speech of the first word of each line. You may wish to type the final draft on a computer.

_____
Title

_____

_____

_____

_____

_____

_____

_____

_____

_____

_____

_____

_____

0-7424-1807-3 Building Grammar & Writing Skills

Name _____ Date _____

Generating Ideas

For most writers, writing is a complex task that is largely a discovery process. Writers create text, review what they have written, and, as a result of the review, generate more ideas. This process is repeated until the project is completed. For fiction writers, many ideas come from what they know best, themselves. Another source writers have for ideas is their own previous writing. They often recycle ideas over and over in different forms. Poems become short stories, and stories become books. Among the many rich resources available to experienced and inexperienced writers alike are personal experiences, previous writing, reading, observation, and conversation. A single piece of writing almost always uses several of these sources.

In the following passage, Benjamin Franklin writes about his youthful mischievous behavior; conduct which, he says, reveals positive qualities that he developed further as an adult. Read the passage, and answer the questions below, discussing responses with classmates.

> I was generally a leader among the boys, and sometimes led them into scrapes, of which I will mention one instance, as it shows an early projecting public spirit, though not then justly conducted. There was a salt-marsh that bounded part of the mill-pond, on the edge of which, at high water, we used to stand to fish for minnows. By much trampling, we had made it a mere quagmire. My proposal was to build a wharf there fit for us to stand upon, and I showed my comrades a large heap of stones, which were intended for a new house near the marsh, and which would very well suit our purpose. Accordingly, in the evening, when the workmen were gone, I assembled a number of my play-fellows, and working with them diligently. . . , sometimes two or three to a stone, we brought them all away and built our little wharf. The next morning the workmen were surprised at missing the stones, which were found in our wharf. Inquiry was made after the removers; we were discovered and complained of; several of us were corrected by our fathers; and though I pleaded the usefulness of the work, mine convinced me that nothing was useful which was not honest.

1. What was Franklin's mischievous behavior?

_____

2. What positive quality of his personality did he think the incident revealed?

_____

3. What valuable lesson did he learn about life?

_____

_____

45

Name _____ Date _____

Rev Up Your Idea Generators

On the lines below, tell of some experience you recall in which you did something you probably shouldn't, but which reveals a positive quality of your personality and taught you a valuable lesson.

1. What was your mischievous behavior?

_____

2. What positive quality of your personality do you think the incident reveals?

_____

3. What valuable lesson did you learn about life?

_____

Now, using the ideas you generated from reading Franklin's essay, the discussions you had with classmates, and the recollections you recorded above, put your experience into a short essay.

_____

_____

_____

_____

_____

_____

_____

_____

_____

_____

_____

_____

_____

_____

Share your experience with classmates.

© McGraw-Hill Children's Publishing

0-7424-1807-3 Building Grammar & Writing Skills

Name _____ Date _____

Planning and Plotting

Although most writers use written plans of some kind, the nature of those plans varies widely from writer to writer. Detailed outlines, charts, pictures, notes, letters, and marginal notations are often used in various combinations. While an outline helps the writer to focus in-depth on a topic and keeps a writer on track, it can also restrict creativity by cutting off the generation of ideas too early. Successful writers often solve this problem by first creating plans and then changing those plans as they think of new and better ideas.

Try your hand at planning the ending of a story that was begun by the English writer Jane Austen when she was young. Read through the story as it is printed here. Then, on the following page, outline the rest of the story as you would conclude it.

One evening in December, as my father, my mother, and myself were arranged in social converse round our fireside, we were, on a sudden, greatly astonished by hearing a violent knocking on the outward door of our rustic cottage.

My father started—"What noise is that," said he.

"It sounds like a loud rapping at the door," replied my mother.

"It does indeed," cried I.

"I am of your opinion," said my father. "It certainly does appear to proceed from some uncommon violence exerted against our unoffending door."

"Yes!" exclaimed I, "I cannot help thinking it must be somebody who knocks for admittance."

"That is another point," replied he. "We must not pretend to determine on what motive the person may knock—tho' that someone *does* rap at the door, I am partly convinced."

Here, a second tremendous rap interrupted my father in his speech, and somewhat alarmed my mother and me.

"Had we not better go and see who it is?" said she. "The servants are out."

"I think we had," replied I.

"Certainly," added my father, "by all means."

"Shall we go now?" said my mother.

"The sooner the better," answered he.

"Oh! Let no time be lost," cried I.

A third, more violent rap than ever, again assaulted our ears.

"I am certain there is somebody knocking at the door," said my mother.

"I think there must," replied my father.

"I fancy the servants are returned," said I. "I think I hear Mary going to the door."

"I'm glad of it," cried my father, "for I long to know who it is."

47

0-7424-1807-3 Building Grammar & Writing Skills

Name _____ Date _____

Sketching Plans

Write a rough outline of your story's conclusion here.

_____

_____

_____

_____

_____

_____

Writers often use sketches to help them plan a piece of writing. Try your hand at sketching the outline you created above. Sketch key events from your story in the order they would occur.

0-7424-1807-3 Building Grammar & Writing Skills

Name _____ Date _____

Drafting

Most successful writers produce a modest number of pages daily, revising as they write. They rarely write for more than a few hours at a time, and they expect periodic episodes of writer's block. To solve the blocking problem, they simply set the material aside for a while and work on something else. Before long they find themselves discovering new ideas, and they continue their writing. Using the outline and sketch that you created on the previous page, draft the conclusion of the story begun by Jane Austen. Be willing to change the outline as you write if you think of better ideas. Don't forget to use the same voice and style, including dialogue, used in the first part of the story. Give the story a title that you think best reflects the content.

Story Title _____

Conclusion of the Story

_____

_____

_____

_____

_____

_____

_____

_____

_____

_____

_____

_____

_____

_____

0-7424-1807-3 Building Grammar & Writing Skills

Name _____ Date _____

Revising

Revision is not something writers do simply to polish a completed draft. Rather, it is a process that begins when a writer writes down the first idea and ends when the last draft is published. During this long process, writers frequently ask friends or coworkers to give their reaction to the work in progress because outside readers are better able to distance themselves from the work and see possible problems. Once a draft is completed, of course, even more intense revision and editing occur. Look over your story conclusion, and ask yourself the following questions:

1. Are there any sentences that sound unnatural or choppy? Where?

_____

2. Does the ending sound as though it were an original part of the story (same voice and style, including dialogue, etc.)?

_____

3. Does the writer use action verbs rather than a lot of linking verbs (*is, are, was, were, etc.*)?

_____

4. Is there any place where you are confused? Where?

_____

5. Is there any place where a reader would need or want more detail? Where?

_____

6. Does the ending fit with the beginning of the story, or does it conflict with earlier events?

_____

7. Are there any problems with punctuation, spelling, or grammar that need to be corrected?

_____

8. Does the title suggest the meaning and events in the story? Why or why not?

_____

Now have two classmates read your story and respond to the same questions, offering explanations for each answer. In response to your readers' suggestions, make whatever changes you feel are appropriate.

Compare versions as all members of the class read their story endings.

0-7424-1807-3 Building Grammar & Writing Skills

Name _____ Date _____

Drawings and Sketches

Manuscripts of many published writers reveal that they used visual aids in their journals and in early drafts. For instance, E. B. White not only drew a sketch of a neighbor's barn but also drew a spider in the corner of an early manuscript page of *Charlotte's Web*. Like published writers, beginning writers find that drawings and sketches help them to organize thoughts and to remember details.

1. Think of a favorite place (a vacation spot, a locker room, the city pool, a movie theater, your backyard, or a dugout). Draw a picture of this place in the space below. On another sheet of paper, write a description of it. Use this description in a story.

2. Ray Bradbury sketched a detailed map of his hometown of Waukegan, Illinois, which he used in *Dandelion Wine*. On another sheet of paper, sketch your neighborhood. Label the streets, homes, and other significant structures. As you label and write, you will find that you recall even more incidents and details. Refer to your neighborhood map for places where memorable events occurred. Use the map or a portion of it for the setting of a story. Describe your setting on the lines below.

_____

_____

_____

_____

_____

_____

_____

_____

_____

_____

© McGraw-Hill Children's Publishing   0-7424-1807-3 Building Grammar & Writing Skills

Name _____ Date _____

Art and Visuals

Our society holds art and visual expression in high esteem. Paintings, pictures, television, videos, and sculptures are among the many methods artists use to express themselves. However, a writer does not have to possess artistic skill to appreciate and use art and visuals as a way to acquire ideas for writing. Many writers refer to pictures and other visual media to help them find topics or expand their topics.

1. John Steinbeck wrote a memorable story called *The Red Pony*. The main character Jody, who longs to ride his horse in the Salinas Rodeo, is based on Steinbeck's childhood experience when he wanted to ride his pony in the rodeo. A picture of Steinbeck on his pony can be found in the Salinas Archives of the Salinas Public Library in Salinas, California. Like Steinbeck, select a childhood photograph of yourself. Examine the photograph carefully and think about why it is special. Create a one-page story using the photograph as a starting point.

2. Cut out pictures from newspapers and magazines that you find particularly interesting; you may create your own file or contribute to a classroom file. Select a picture. Describe your picture on the lines below.

_____

_____

_____

_____

Now "read" the picture and write one or two pages, telling the picture's story. Share the picture and the story with the class.

3. Visuals can help writers expand their descriptions. Find pictures of the faces of people from all walks of life, both males and females. Large pictures with a front view work best. Cut out the pictures, trimming away everything but the eyes. If the person is identified, you may wish to write the name on the back of the picture. Select one picture. Carefully examine the eyes and describe them on the lines below with detail: arch of eyebrows; size, shape, and color; whether they are squinting, narrow, glaring, etc. You may wish to do the same with other facial features.

_____

_____

_____

_____

Write a characterization using this description. You most likely will notice that your description expands "he has blue eyes"—a description many beginning writers feel is sufficient.

0-7424-1807-3 Building Grammar & Writing Skills

Name _____ Date _____

Personal Experiences

When asked about idea generation, published writers indicate that they get their topics from a variety of sources, but those sources fall into common categories. Those categories include real people, real places, and real experiences from one's travels, childhood, jobs, and even dreams.

Below is a list of experience categories from which published writers find specific topics. In the space provided in the right-hand column, provide brief details about a specific personal experience for each of the categories.

Experience	Specific Topics and Details
People	
Places	
Travel	
Childhood	
Jobs	
Dreams	

From this chart select an experience topic and write a narrative essay. You may wish to expand the project to include several incidents in a longer work.

0-7424-1807-3 Building Grammar & Writing Skills

Name _____ Date _____

Avid Readers = Imaginative Writers

Experienced writers tend to be avid readers. They often express a great love for all types of print media. They commonly surround themselves with books, and they subscribe to many magazines. From their reading they take notes, which they use to expand their lists of writing ideas. Their writing then often becomes a mix of their own ideas and inspiration from their reading. One author who practiced reading and note-taking religiously was Jack London. His library contained thousands of books, many of which London annotated with carefully written notes.

Sometimes nonfiction can provide inspiration for fictional works. For example, current events in newspaper and magazine articles may contain people, places, and events that would make interesting characters, settings, and plots.

Find an interesting article in a newspaper or magazine. On the lines below jot down details about the following:

Article Title _____

Source _____ Publication Date _____

Person _____

_____

_____

Place _____

_____

_____

Event _____

_____

_____

_____

Form a small group and share your notes with group members. Like London, select a person, place, and event from one or more articles to use as inspiration for a short story. Use the nonfiction source as inspiration. Do not copy passages word for word and insert them into your story. Rather, use the source as a way of recalling your own similar experience, which you combine with details from the source. Share your story with members of your group.

0-7424-1807-3 Building Grammar & Writing Skills

Name _____ Date _____

Original Research

Experienced writers are curious about their surroundings and are attentive to details. Consequently, they are always using their observation skills. Recognizing problems is one type of observation that provides writers with many topics.

Problems exist everywhere. Think of two problems in your neighborhood, in your school, in your city, or in your state. For example, a problem in your school may have to do with decreased funding for extracurricular activities; a problem in your state may have to do with an environmental issue, such as increased pollutants from large industries.

Problems

1. _____

2. _____

Select one of the problems. On the lines below describe this problem as though you were explaining it to someone else.

_____

_____

_____

_____

_____

_____

_____

_____

Share your writing with a partner and ask your partner for suggestions on how it can be solved. List possible ways to solve the problem below.

1. _____

2. _____

3. _____

On another sheet of paper, list steps to take to solve the problem, along with the people and money that would be needed to accomplish the task. Then, think of a person or group who has some authority to implement your solution. Write a letter explaining the problem and offering your solutions.

Name _____ Date _____

Library Research

Many experienced writers report extensive use of the library. Before writing *The Red Badge of Courage*, Stephen Crane reportedly spent a year researching Civil War books and magazines. Ray Bradbury read Sara Teasdale's poem "There Will Come Soft Rains" and later wrote a short story by the same name.

Become familiar with your school and/or community library. Think of nonfiction topics you would enjoy researching in the library. They may include specific animals, rocks and minerals, advances in medical research, historical figures, sports history, technical advances, or political events. List two topics below.

I. _____

2. _____

Find three or four books or articles in the library about your topic. Create an annotated file of your research, using the form below. A large file of notes will give a wide variety of topics and details.

Title

Author

Notes

Page number _____

Write a short story from your notes. Your notes will become extremely important as you write. For example, you would have to know the habits of the starfish if a starfish appears in your story. You would need to know the particulars about a city (temperature, population) if using it as a setting.

Place the stories in a classroom anthology.

© McGraw-Hill Children's Publishing 0-7424-1807-3 Building Grammar & Writing Skills

Name _____ Date _____

Narrowing the Focus

After selecting a general topic, experienced writers realize that they must think about exactly what they wish to say about that topic. For example, you may choose a topic about which you are extremely interested and about which you already know a lot of information, or about which you can find a lot of information. In either case, the abundance of information may be overwhelming and difficult to organize. If this occurs, you will need to limit your topic to one that fits the needs of your audience and of your purpose.

Think about the following when narrowing the focus of your topic:
1. What is my purpose in writing?
2. Who is my intended audience?
3. What type of document will I produce?
4. What is the probable length of the paper?
5. How long do I have to finish the project?

The following topics are too general. For each general topic, list a topic that has a narrower focus. Then, on the second line, describe a situation (audience and occasion) where this information would be welcome. The first one has been done for you.

1. Birds   the nesting habits of eagles
                a meeting of a bird watcher's club

2. Cooking _____

_____

3. Explorers _____

_____

4. Music _____

_____

Select a topic that interests you. Keep narrowing its focus until it becomes limited enough to fit a particular audience and purpose. The narrowed topic will be more specific and more concrete.

Topic _____

Narrowed Topic _____

Audience and Purpose _____

     0-7424-1807-3 Building Grammar & Writing Skills

Name _____ Date _____

Creating Titles and Headings

Titles and headings appear to be important tools for published writers. Students often need to be reminded to give their papers titles when they turn in essays, but some published writers seem to have been unable to proceed or even to begin without them. The title appears to serve as a guide. By providing a key phrase that describes both the possibilities and the limitations of the writing project, the title becomes functional and not merely decorative. The title encourages writers to think globally about their writing, yet enables them to keep focused on the topic.

In technical writing headings help the reader follow the order of information. Like titles of creative texts, headings of technical documents supply the reader with a clear idea of what follows.

1. Read the titles of some well-known creative works. Then imitate the titles by creating your own original titles, using similar parts of speech. Four examples follow with the parts of speech in parentheses.

Anne of Green Gables [proper noun + prepositional phrase]
Holes [plural noun]
"The Highwayman" [article + noun]
Little Women [adjective + noun]

Found Title _____ Your Title _____

Found Title _____ Your Title _____

2. Informative documents often contain headings, which help readers stay focused on the document. Create headings for a student research paper on literature. Use the details below to create an appropriate heading for each section.

Section 1: description of factual works, with definitions of biography, autobiography, and informative articles
Section 2: discussion of creative works, including short stories, novels, folktales, and myths
Section 3: definitions and samples of haiku, ballads, sonnets, and lyrical poems
Section 4: information about skits, one-act plays, Shakespearean tragedies, and musicals

Section 1 _____

Section 2 _____

Section 3 _____

Section 4 _____

 0-7424-1807-3 Building Grammar & Writing Skills

Name _____ Date _____

Using Graphic Organizers

To maintain focus many writers organize their thoughts visually on the page. In writing classes this visual representation is commonly referred to as a *graphic organizer*. There are numerous types of graphic organizers, including Venn diagrams, T-bars, and webs.

Organizers are helpful because they encourage writers to think about their topic before actually writing. They help writers avoid jumping into first drafts prematurely only to find that they do not have enough to say or that they do not know exactly what they want to say. Writers can also see the order at a glance and add details as they write.

Notice how the student writer completed the T-bar organizer below. On the left she organized information in the order she wanted to present it. On the right, she listed her feelings and reactions next to the corresponding event on the left.

Title: **A Time When Hard Work Paid Off**

Neighbors asked to care for dogs while they were on vacation	Happy/excited they wanted me
Day 1: fed and walked no problem	Felt that the job would mean easy money
Day 2: fed, groomed, walked no problem	Time-consuming and boring
Day 3: golden retriever got loose nervous; thought about options looked for hours: neighborhood yards uptown streets posted signs	Worried about what they would say
Found dog next day	Extremely relieved
Neighbors returned, gave bonus, and referred me to their friends	Looking back, proud I kept searching and stayed with the job

On another sheet of paper, create a T-bar. Complete both sides of it choosing a topic of your own or using one of the following topics: a time when hard work paid off; a time when hard work did not pay off; a time when you were embarrassed; a time when you were proud. Then write the narrative. In small groups read the narratives and discuss how the graphic organizer helped you follow the order of events and stay focused as you wrote.

Name _____ Date _____

Writing Outlines

A traditional outline, either topic or sentence, organizes your information into main topics and subtopics. Writers often prefer an outline rather than a graphic organizer when writing longer documents.

Standard guidelines require that main topics follow Roman numerals, that subtopics follow capital letters, and that supporting details follow Arabic numerals. Parallel structure within each division (if *A* begins with a verb, *B, C,* and *D* should also begin with verbs) helps maintain focus. The traditional requirement of at least two topics, subtopics, or details within a section (if there is a *I*, there must be a *II*, if there is an *A*, there must be a *B*) helps the writer see whether there is enough support and if the support is balanced throughout the sections.

Study the sample outline and complete the outline to the right using the title, main topics, subtopics, and supporting details below.

Title of Essay	Title _____
I. Main Topic	I. _____
A. Subtopic	A. _____
B. Subtopic	B. _____
C. Subtopic	C. _____
1. Supporting detail	1. _____
2. Supporting detail	2. _____
3. Supporting detail	3. _____
II. Main Topic	II. _____
A. Subtopic	A. _____
1. Supporting detail	1. _____
2. Supporting detail	2. _____
B. Subtopic	B. _____
1. Supporting detail	1. _____
2. Supporting detail	2. _____

Title   Ways to Eliminate Stress

Main Topics   Exercise, Organize

Subtopics   Anaerobic, Rearrange folders, Clean locker, Aerobic, Make lists of due dates

Supporting Details   Swimming, Yoga, Assignments, Quizzes and tests, Jogging, Weight lifting, Other obligations

    0-7424-1807-3 Building Grammar & Writing Skills

Name _____ Date _____

Building Your Case

Most students find it helpful to see an example of a finished product before they have to submit a similar one. Likewise, readers appreciate examples when they read. Examples are verbal illustrations that demonstrate a general statement. They serve to prove the writer's opinions with specific support. When writers prove ideas with supporting examples, they clarify and lend credibility to their topics. To signal that an example follows, writers include such phrases as *for instance* and *for example*.

Select the two best examples for the following topic by placing an *X* in front of two of them.

Topic: Many small children learn lessons the hard way—by first-hand experience.

_____ My mother told my sister not to touch the hot stove. She did anyway. Not only did she cry, but her index finger blistered from the burn.

_____ When she was three, my sister paddled around in a lifejacket at the lake.

_____ When we returned the next year, she thought she could swim and jumped off the dock without the lifejacket. My dad had to jump in and rescue her.

_____ Yesterday a friend repeated something I told her in confidence. I'm still upset.

_____ My older sister helps me with difficult homework assignments.

_____ My younger brother practiced pitching every day last summer. His friend didn't practice at all but was selected as the starting pitcher in the Little People's League. My brother said, "Life isn't fair!"

Discuss with a partner why you selected those that you did and why you did not select the others. Then, with your partner, think of three examples for each of the following topics.

1. Some people enjoy seeing movies at the theater instead of renting them on video or DVD to watch at home. Movies in theaters have sharper images and better sound.

_____   _____   _____

2. I prefer reading books in a series because I get to see characters develop and the plot is more involved.

_____   _____   _____

3. I do not purchase every new item advertised because fads go out of style so quickly.

_____   _____   _____

On another sheet of paper, write an essay supporting one of these topics using the examples you have chosen.

61

Name _____ Date _____

Facts and Statistics

Facts are another way writers can support their topics. Facts indicate that the writer has done research, giving the writer credibility as a knowledgeable source. Technical writers must always be certain that their documents contain correct information. For instance, names must be spelled correctly and statistics must be accurate. Common ways to collect facts are through surveys and observation.

Surveys. In surveys the writer collects information by designing questions, collecting responses (by telephone, in person, by mail, by e-mail), and analyzing the data. For example, if you wanted to know whether middle school students prefer adding a bowling team or debate team to the school's extracurricular activities, you would poll students.

Observation. Careful observation or monitoring sometimes is the best way to gather supporting information. For instance, to gather facts you may wish to observe the eating habits of a hedgehog or the growth of geraniums in two different types of soil.

Charts and graphs are good visuals to include with the written explanation of surveys and observations. Examples include pie charts, bar graphs, line graphs, and tables.

Conduct one of the following surveys and one of the following observational studies.

1. Conduct a survey concerning the types of assignments middle school students prefer: worksheets, open-ended essay questions, speeches, or computer-based (Internet searches and/or use of word processing software). Write a one-page report supporting your topic with information from your survey.

2. Conduct a survey to find out what types of media people of various ages prefer. Determine age groups and ask members from each age group whether they prefer to read print materials (novels, nonfiction books, magazines, newspapers), surf the Internet, watch television, or listen to the radio. Write a one-page report supporting your topic with information from your survey.

3. Conduct an observational study. Closely examine how students interact with one another: in the hallways, in the classrooms, in physical education class, during extracurricular activities, and in the cafeteria. Write notes describing exactly what you see. Then write a one-page report supporting your topic with significant facts.

4. Observe the behavior of an animal: a classroom pet, a pet at home, or even wild birds in your backyard. List all behaviors over a period of several days. Then complete a one-page report supporting your topic with information from your observations.

0-7424-1807-3 Building Grammar & Writing Skills

Name _____ Date _____

Evocative and Instructive Description

Experienced writers realize that description is more than filler; description supports topics by making them come alive through details. Description supports both narrative and expository writing but in different ways. In narrative writing, description serves to evoke an emotion; in technical writing, description serves to clarify instructions.

Narrative Writing. In narrative writing writers consider all the senses (sight, sound, taste, smell, and touch) and use them to produce an overall emotion. For example, description of a circus may evoke the emotion of excitement. It should evoke the senses:

Sight	trapeze act, elephants, clowns with colored balloons
Sound	people milling, vendors calling for business, announcements
Taste	ice cream, fried dough, cotton candy
Smell	popcorn popping, straw, animals
Touch	seat in big tent, string of a balloon, texture of cotton candy

1. Select one of the following topics and emotions. Write a passage describing the place you have chosen, including all the senses that help to evoke the emotion you have selected.

Topic		**Emotion**	
woods	basement	pride	loneliness
cabin	gymnasium	sadness	nervousness
city street	busy store	happiness	fear

Technical Writing. Technical writers frequently describe how things work or give instructions concerning how to do something. Accuracy and clarity rather than emotions are essential when writing technical descriptions. Emotions do not appear in technical descriptions.

2. List words and phrases that describe one of the following objects. Compare your list of words with those of a classmate who chose the same object. From your combined lists, choose words and phrases that best describe the object. Together write a description of this item. Be certain that your description is accurate, clear, and objective (contains no emotions).

garden rake	blender	music reed	ink pen
curling iron	stopwatch	flashlight	paper clip
scissors	fishing reel	can opener	button

3. Give step-by-step instructions on how to use one of the following tools. As with your technical description, concentrate on accuracy, clarity, and objectivity.

pliers	screwdriver	putty knife	pencil sharpener
hammer	wrench	crowbar	level

Name _____ Date _____

Quotations in Narrative Writing

Narrative writing, which includes short stories, novels, biographies, and autobiographies, almost always contains dialogue between two or more characters. Three signals alert readers to quotations in narrative writing: separate paragraphs, quotation marks, and introductory phrases or "tags," such as *he said*, *she asked*, and *I shouted*.

In narrative writing authors sometimes choose to include introductory phrases identifying the speaker or source of information, and at other times they choose to omit them. When writers omit them, new paragraphs and quotation marks are sufficient to tell the reader who is speaking. Tags can be omitted if the conversation is short or if only two people are speaking.

I. Give your reader clear signals concerning who is speaking in the following conversation. Rewrite the conversation. Use quotations marks around each speaker's words, and change paragraphs every time the speaker changes. Use tags where necessary. In places where the speaker is apparent through other signals, leave out the tags.

It all came about one day when my mom asked would you boys like to take a ride? Sure we said. Where are we going? We're going to run the lawn mower to the shop for repairs my mother replied. Mom, is it okay if Aaron and I get a maze book and some treats on the way? Well, okay, and you better pick up a package of pencils too.

_____

_____

_____

_____

_____

_____

_____

_____

2. On another sheet of paper, write a narrative that includes a dialogue between two or more characters. Change paragraphs each time you change speakers. Use quotation marks around each speaker's words. When needed, include introductory tags to clarify which character is speaking.

Name _____ Date _____

Quotations in Expository Writing

Words of an expert in any field carry authority; therefore, many writers include words of experts in their own writing. Such statements often appear in research reports in the form of direct quotations. Direct quotations should be copied exactly—word for word with no alteration or error. Since report writing contains much information obtained from other sources in the form of quotations, introductory tags are especially important. To clarify the source of the quotation, the writer may introduce the quotation with a phrase such as *"according to Ryan Wright . . ."* or *"Molecular researcher Ryan Wright says. . . ."*

Read the following excerpt from a student report about the writing process of Herman Melville.
   Author Dorothy Ruth says, "The manuscript materials available for *Billy Budd* are particularly rich, providing insight into all phases of its composition, including Melville's prewriting, his drafting, and his revising" (9).

The student writer gives credit to the quotation by including the source of the quotation, Dorothy Ruth, and the page number (9) upon which the quotation appears. This information helps the reader learn about the publication in which the quotation originally appeared. By looking at the end of the student research paper, the reader finds a list of works the student consulted while writing the paper. In the above instance, the entry in the list of works would appear as follows:
   Ruth, Dorothy. "Resource Materials for *Billy Budd.*" *Literature and Writing*, Feb. 1988: 9–14.

Read the following quotations and answer the questions that follow.
   Available manuscripts do not exist for Emily Bronte's novel *Wuthering Heights*. According to Mary Peters, "Bronte's earlier writing that may have served as preparation for *Wuthering Heights* primarily included her early poetry" (14).

1. Who is the expert source? _____

2. Copy the introductory tag. _____

3. On which page number does the quotation appear? _____

   Ann Karel, a noted Dickens researcher says, "Charles Dickens found that physical exercise helped him avoid the energy drain resulting from the intense emotional and physical requirements of writing" (7).

1. Who is the expert source? _____

2. Copy the introductory tag. _____

3. On which page number does the quotation appear? _____

65

Name _____ Date _____

Paraphrases in Expository Writing

Another way report writers include information from other sources is to paraphrase. Since a paraphrase does not contain the exact words of the original source, the writer omits the quotation marks. However, the writer still uses a tag to introduce and to identify the original information, and still follows the passage with the page number in parentheses.

The following paragraph contains a paraphrase of a passage from an original source.
    According to Dorothy Ruth, many writers emphasize the importance of order in their daily writing routines, as though control of some parts of the physical environment compensates for the chaotic nature of writing itself. The significance of such routines lies not in the writer's individual behaviors but in their adherence to established practices (11).

The above information was found on page 11 of *Writing With the Masters: From Personal Experiences*. The student writer did not copy Dorothy Ruth's words exactly but still gives credit to the author and includes the page number on which the information appears.

Read the following exact quotation. On the lines that follow, paraphrase the quotation. Begin with the introductory tag to name the source of your information. Add the page number of your source in the parentheses at the end.
    "Golden retrievers love activity—running, climbing, swimming, digging, and fetching. But they especially love being petted and sitting quietly at their master's feet or by the fire. Golden retrievers are strong, fast, loyal, calm, and predictable. As a result, they are one of the favorite breeds for guide, military, and police work." Author: Mary Peters; Source: *Writing for the Real World*, page 109.

_____

_____

_____

_____

_____

_____

0-7424-1807-3 Building Grammar & Writing Skills

Name _____ Date _____

Organizational Patterns

The structural patterns that you choose when you write are determined by what you want to say. At various times in your school writing, you may be given formulas for writing. One such form is the popular "five-paragraph theme," which often works well in a testing situation, but tends to restrict the generation of creative ideas. In fact, some readers of college entrance exams dismiss such formulaic essays as evidence of a writer's lack of real thought. Obviously, not all topics in the world come in three parts (introduction, three development paragraphs, and a conclusion). While different writing situations have many things in common, no single formula is going to work in all cases. Each piece of writing needs to have an organizational design that fits the topic, the writer's purpose, and the reader's expectations.

Below are five commonly used organizational patterns: cause/effect, chronological order, comparison/contrast, problem/solution, and topics. Sometimes these patterns govern the overall structure of a piece of writing, and sometimes they govern only parts of a piece of writing. For example, an overall structure that is organized chronologically may have individual paragraphs developed with topical, cause/effect, or some other pattern. Recall the worst book you ever read. Think about how you might organize a paragraph about this experience using each of the structural patterns below. Briefly describe how each could be used. The first one is done for you. (Suggestions for possible ways of developing other patterns are given in parentheses.)

cause/effect: usually shows how one cause has several effects, or several causes have one effect
   I'd say that when people make students read horrible books like that, they want to stop
   reading books at all and just go to movies instead.

chronological order: presents events in time sequence (What was the book? What happened?)

_____

comparison/contrast: shows similarities or differences in two or more related things
(How is another book on a similar topic or by the same author better than the hateful book?)

_____

problem/solution: offers one or more solutions to an existing problem
(What can teachers do to avoid making students have bad reading experiences?)

_____

topics: give a general statement followed by a list of reasons, examples, illustrations
(Teachers should not assign these kinds of books because of 1. ..., 2. ..., 3. ..., etc.)

_____

Choose one of these patterns and write a paragraph about your unpleasant book experience.

67

Name _____ Date _____

Organizing a Report

As you have seen, there are various ways to organize material, depending on the point you want to make. In the following assignment, you will be asked to find out about your community's cultural background and organize your findings in a written and oral report. You will need to decide what organizational pattern will work best for your information and your audience.

Conduct an interview of students in the school or other people in the community whose families came to this country as immigrants. To add to your report, you may want to ask the Chamber of Commerce or local historical group for further information. Be certain to include your own responses to the questions also, so that your family's heritage is included in your community's cultural snapshot. Create a set of interview questions, such as

- Where did your family come from?
- What was life like there?
- Why did the family come to this country?
- How is this country different?
- How is it the same?
- What would you like people in this country to understand about your native country?
- About immigrants?

Write a report to share with the class, providing the following information:

> The people you interviewed
> The questions you asked
> The people's responses
> Generalizations you can make about the community based on these responses

You could organize this report in various ways. For example, you could put the responses of individual people into separate sections. Or you could have separate sections for each of the four categories above (the people you interviewed, the questions you asked, the people's responses, and your generalizations). Within each section, you would want to group responses together when appropriate (such as reasons for coming, similarities to native country, differences from native country, and what people should understand about immigrants). You will want to add a short introductory paragraph, telling why it is important to know the contributions of various cultural groups to the community, and a brief concluding paragraph telling why this was a useful and informative project.

Once you have gathered your information and written a draft, go on to the next activity page to make your report clearer to the reader by using headings and other structural cues.

   0-7424-1807-3 Building Grammar & Writing Skills

Name _____ Date _____

Structural Cues

Headings and Titles. In addition to having an appropriate overall pattern, your readers benefit greatly when you provide structural cues, such as informative titles, section headings, and word cues throughout the piece of writing. Titles and headings can be very helpful to readers by showing where each section begins and ends. Furthermore, they break up the visual monotony, making the writing more reader friendly. Headings are most helpful when they are brief, clear, and directly related to content. The same is true for titles, which should tell the reader something important about the writing. Look at your report on immigrants. Put headings where you think they can help the reader. For example, you might have headings such as these:

Countries Represented in Local Community
Immigrants' Reasons for Coming to the United States
Similarities to the United States
Differences from the United States
Contributions of Immigrants to Local Community
What U.S. Citizens Need to Understand About Immigrants

Using Word Cues to Indicate Structure. Once you have arranged the content in appropriate sections, you will want to provide signposts along the way to help readers make connections between and within paragraphs and sentences. Conjunctions are some of the most common cue words that we use. They tell whether a second idea should be added (*and*), contrasted (*but, yet*), seen as a cause (*for*), or seen as an alternative (*or*). Many other words and phrases are also used to signal structure. Some common ones are *however, as a result, consequently, finally, for example, furthermore, in addition, meanwhile, similarly, on the other hand, until, then, because of this, another, furthermore, in other words,* and *therefore.* Read through your report on immigrants to see where you can add word cues to make the report more reader friendly.

Using Punctuation to Indicate Structure. Even punctuation provides signals to your reader about your structural plan at the sentence level. For example, if you set something off in commas or put something in parentheses, your reader knows that you are providing interesting, but probably not essential, information (something like a whispered aside). Commas coming before a coordinating conjunction (*and, or, nor, but, for, so, yet*) tell the reader that a complete thought will follow. Again, look through your report to be certain that you have used punctuation appropriately and that it helps to guide the reader smoothly through the report.

Presenting an Oral Report. When you have finished writing your report, create an oral presentation to share with classmates. You will want to use visual aids to display the responses. For example, you may want to list all of the represented countries on the board and show them on a map of the world. If people you interviewed had artifacts to share, you could show them to the class. As class members present their findings, compile results on a large poster, creating a composite picture of the community.

69

Name _____ Date _____

Testing Situations

Topical Essays. In testing situations, when you have little time to generate ideas and revise them, you may be wise to use a stock formula, such as the five-paragraph topical essay, which begins with a generalization followed by examples or reasons (usually three). In fact, the test itself may require this format. In such instances, the writer usually

   1. begins with an introductory statement telling readers the point of the essay;

   2. offers three reasons/examples;

   3. concludes by restating the point made in the introduction.

Thomas Jefferson once said, "Nothing is troublesome that we do willingly." Think about times when you have done things willingly and those times you have resented having to do something. Was it easier when you were willing? Write an essay that either agrees or disagrees with Jefferson. Outline your essay here, and write a draft on a separate sheet of paper.

_____

_____

_____

_____

_____

Narrative Essays. Another common test format is the narrative essay, recounting some memorable event in chronological order. In this case, the introduction and conclusion are similar to those in the topical essay, but the middle paragraphs recount events in the experience.

   1. begins with an introductory statement telling readers the point of the essay

   2. recounts pertinent details of the event in the order they happened

   3. concludes by restating the point made in the introduction

Another of Thomas Jefferson's recommendations was "When angry count ten before you speak; if very angry, a hundred." Think of a time when you failed to follow Jefferson's advice—you spoke and later wished you hadn't. Or think of a time when you did follow his advice and kept quiet. Write the outline here for this narrative. On a separate sheet of paper, write the essay.

_____

_____

_____

_____

_____

70

Name _____ Date _____

Do You Hear Me?

Most of the writing you do outside the classroom is geared for a specific audience—the reader or readers of your work. You also write for a specific purpose—how you want readers to react. A third factor to consider is your voice, which has to do with what the readers learn about you personally in the way you write. Depending on your audience and purpose, you may want readers to feel that they know you well, or you may want them to focus instead on the ideas. In the following essay, the student writer skillfully conveys personal voice in her writing. When you finish reading it, you almost feel that you know her personally. Expressive essays like this are often written for writing contests, where screening committees look for pieces that show not only the writer's ability to develop a topic, but also tell something about the writer. Read the essay and answer the questions on the following page.

Reflections Upon the Death of a Friend, by Alena Green

My gray station wagon has been more than a car to me. Today it suffered an untimely (not to mention inconvenient) death. The slow decline had been going on for years. Bought extremely used in 1988, our wagon was a hard old veteran when it reached my family. As a stolen vehicle repossession, it made us marvel at what kind of hoodlum would steal a Chevy Caprice classic full-sized wagon.

Being a repo didn't matter to the six-year-old Alena, though. I remember the excitement I felt when my parents picked me up from kindergarten in this gray behemoth. A "mother ship" is what my sister called it. The "old gray wagon" is what the rest of us said. It transported me from tee ball games and 4-H meetings, stunning victories and bitter defeats. The smell of dust and moldy childhood substances were permanently stuck in its cloth interior.

As my sister came of age, it became an emblem of excitement. Decorated with glow-in-the-dark stars and the stickers of rock bands, it transported me to school by a means other than the bus, which was, to my junior high mentality, absolute freedom. I can still picture Sonya coming up the lane, her small frame barely recognizable as she pluckily handled the giant automobile.

With the influence of Sonya, however, the car began to realize its limitations. A permanent chugging sound now accompanied any acceleration. Various fender benders suffered at her inexperienced hands also shortened my dear wagon's life. By the time I was ready to drive, the air conditioner had to be temporarily shut off if you required enough oomph to pass. (A very necessary function for teenaged drivers.) The ceiling on the passenger's side, once brightly decorated, now lay sagging to the point of messing up Anton's hair.

We all knew that our friend was on its last leg. But it still greeted me as a shock when my father announced that the wagon was no longer fit for consistent use. She was to be put out to pasture, used only for the shortest and least taxing trips. The old gray station wagon, more than toting me around for twelve years, had defined my existence. She served as an e-mail address (greywagon@aol), a class float (she was elected class car for the homecoming parade our sophomore year), and ultimately, an attention-getting mechanism—the ultimate tool in the Green family. I will miss the car that gave me an identity in the world of uniform, mid-sized vehicles.

71

Name _____ Date _____

Analyzing Voice

As readers, we react partly to the content, but we react also to the personality or voice that we hear in the writing. The stronger the personality coming through a piece, the stronger our reaction. Sometimes we react negatively. Other times we respond with humor, sympathy, or understanding, as though we have had a shared experience or an intimate conversation.

1. What kind of person do you visualize as the author of "Reflections Upon the Death of a Friend"? Describe her.

_____

_____

_____

2. What passages do you respond to most strongly? List several and explain why these struck a special chord for you.

_____

_____

_____

Write a short essay, similar to the one written by the student writer, in which you tell of some treasured object. Make your personality show through. Share your essay with classmates, asking them to comment on how successful you have been at letting your voice come through.

Title _____

_____

_____

_____

_____

_____

_____

_____

0-7424-1807-3 Building Grammar & Writing Skills

Name _____ Date _____

Impersonal Idea Delivery

In some writing tasks, you do not want readers to think about you personally. You want them to focus instead on the ideas. The following piece of writing—in contrast to the previous essay in which you got to know the writer quite well—has little evidence of personal voice, except for a slight sense of humor. The assignment was to summarize a fairy tale, retaining key points. The audience was the teacher. Notice how little you can tell about the personality of this writer.

The Emperor's New Clothes
Adapted from Hans Christian Andersen

Once there was a very vain king who was particularly fond of fine clothing. When two con artists posing as weavers convinced him that they could produce clothing for him that was both more beautiful than anyone else's and visible only to intelligent people, he fell for the scam and ordered production of the clothes in spite of their great expense to his kingdom.

When the weavers finally dressed the emperor in his new clothes, the courtiers assured their king that his clothing was quite fetching, in spite of the fact that they could see he was quite naked. The commoners in his kingdom, on the other hand, were less charitable (or gullible). When he paraded publicly, their response convinced him that he had, indeed, been duped and quite exposed.

Write your own summary of a favorite fairy tale. Although you may want to interject a little humor, keep your personal voice at a minimum. Focus instead on key points in the story.

Title _____

Summary _____

_____

_____

_____

_____

_____

_____

_____

_____

_____

73

Name _____ Date _____

Business and Technical Writing Tones

Writers in the business world use even less personal voice than that in the fairy tale revision. Business writers want readers to focus entirely on the subject matter, not at all on the person writing it. Note the absence of voice in the following letter from an Internet provider. The audience is their customers; the purpose is to inform customers of an interruption in the service.

Dear Customer:

Your Internet service will be interrupted for six hours tomorrow for routine maintenance and upgrading of the system. The system will go down at 11:00 P.M., and service will be restored at 5:00 A.M. If further work is necessary, you will be notified. If you have questions, call Customer Service at 1-800-000-0000, extension 5014.

Sincerely,

Following the example of the business letter above, write a notice to students in your school from the custodial staff, giving students the following information:
- The gymnasium will be unavailable to clubs and sports activities.
- The floor is going to be refinished.
- Refinishing starts next week.
- Students need to use the north door of the building.
- Gymnasium doors will be locked.
- The job will take two weeks.

_____

_____

_____

_____

_____

_____

_____

_____

_____

0-7424-1807-3 Building Grammar & Writing Skills

Name _____ Date _____

Know Your Audience

In any piece of writing, you need to tailor what you write for a particular audience—the intended reader. Sometimes this reader may be someone close to you, such as a favorite aunt; other times it may be someone who does not know you at all, such as a high school counselor at a new school wanting to place you in the most appropriate writing class. Questions you need to ask yourself about your audience include: (1) What do the readers already know? (2) What do the readers still need to know? (3) What will persuade the readers to take me seriously?

Example #1. Suppose that a local theater has discontinued student rates on tickets and has raised the prices on popcorn and candy. The Student Council decides to protest the price hikes by writing a letter to the company. They consider each of the questions above.

1. The company knows that this is the only movie theater in town, and teenagers are their best customers.

2. The company needs to know that two theaters in a neighboring town have lower prices, and parents have agreed to drive students to movies in the neighboring town.

3. The company may be persuaded with information about the exact costs in the neighboring theaters, showing them that the students are serious and have done their homework on this issue.

What other information would you include in this letter if you were trying to convince the movie company to change their minds about the price hikes? Discuss responses with classmates.

_____

Example #2. The freshman class has asked permission from the City Council to hold a car wash at the city park to make money. Neighboring car wash facilities complain about the competition. As secretary of the freshman class, to whom would you write a letter? Answer the audience analysis questions; then discuss your answers with classmates.

Who is the audience? _____

What do they already know? _____

What do they need to know? _____

What will persuade them to take the writer seriously? _____

Write one of these letters, either the letter to the movie company or the one about the car wash. Include additional information that might persuade the audience to see things your way. Read one another's papers. Ask readers whether they would be convinced if they were the audience.

75

Name _____ Date _____

Know Your Purpose

Along with knowing the audience's needs and expectations, writers must understand their own purposes. They need to know exactly what they want to happen as a result of the writing. Below is a list of writers and audiences. Think of possible purposes for writing in each of these instances. The first one is done for you.

1. A middle school student is writing an e-mail message to a good friend in another city. Possible purpose To ask the friend to come for a visit during summer vacation _____

2. A paper carrier is writing a note to a customer on her route.

Possible purpose _____

3. A member of the soccer team is writing a letter to members of the Board of Education.

Possible purpose _____

4. A mother or father is writing a note to a teacher.

Possible purpose _____

5. A teacher is writing a letter to a father or mother.

Possible purpose _____

Write a short paragraph on the topic of pets. First, identify your audience, your purpose, and the voice you want to convey (a strong personal voice or a detached, impersonal voice).

Audience _____

Purpose _____

Voice _____

_____

_____

_____

_____

_____

_____

_____

_____

76

Name _____ Date _____

Technetronic Research

Every day more and more people rely on technology to create and disseminate information. If you have access to the Internet, you have a vast resource for generating information on all types of topics. You can even publish your work on-line. The projects on pages 77–82 require the use of technology to find information on a wide range of subjects. After generating your information, you will publish some of your findings by presenting them to an audience of your peers using visual aids, such as PowerPoint if it is available, and to an Internet audience on one of the Web's many sites for publishing student work.

Literary Figures. Many famous authors have had their letters and diaries published. Although the diaries and letters may not have been meant for publication when they were written, they enable us now to learn a lot about these famous writers—how they got their ideas, how they worked, and what they thought. Find letters or journal entries of famous authors on the Internet. Read at least three letters or journal entries, and briefly describe the contents on the lines below.

Author's Name _____

Internet Location _____

Letter or Journal Entry #1

_____

_____

_____

Letter or Journal Entry #2

_____

_____

_____

Letter or Journal Entry #3

_____

_____

_____

What did you find out? Write a one-page report telling what you learned about this author by reading these personal letters and journal entries. Share your findings with the class.

 0-7424-1807-3 Building Grammar & Writing Skills

Name _____ Date _____

Gathering History

Working in small groups, choose a period in history to research. Use the Internet, computer databases, library, family members, people in the community, television programs and documentaries, etc., to find out all you can about what life was like in that period. Look at science, art, literature, transportation, music, politics, methods of farming, major industries, fashion, food, hairstyles, and social customs of the time. Fill in the information below and on page 79 to guide your search.

Time period _____

Political environment (war, peace) _____

_____

_____

_____

Economic environment (depression, financial upswing) _____

_____

_____

_____

Scientific advancements _____

_____

_____

_____

Transportation (types of cars or other modes of transportation) _____

_____

_____

_____

Health/medicine (advancements, concerns) _____

_____

_____

_____

Popular culture (radio, TV, movies, celebrities) _____

_____

_____

_____

continue on next page

0-7424-1807-3 Building Grammar & Writing Skills

Name _____ Date _____

Gathering History, Continued

Sports and sports figures _____
_____
_____

Literature popular during the period _____
_____
_____

Music/dance/art _____
_____
_____

Means of making a living for the average person (farming, factories, etc.) _____
_____
_____

Schools (types of public schools and average level of education) _____
_____
_____

Fashion and hairstyles _____
_____
_____

Social customs specific to the period _____
_____
_____

Prepare written and oral reports by grouping the above categories into larger topics with headings such as *arts and entertainment, political and scientific environment, school and work,* and *social environment.* In your report, include specific details and stories to illustrate important features of the historical period. Provide sound and visual information where appropriate. If possible, video-tape each group's presentations. Publish your report on one of the many Internet sites that publish student work.

0-7424-1807-3 Building Grammar & Writing Skills

Name _____ Date _____

Tours in Cyberspace

Work in small groups to plan an exotic journey. Think of a place out of this country that you would like to visit if you could. Imagine that you have been given time, money, and tickets to go there. Plan a two-week itinerary for your trip. Go to the Internet to find out what the climate is like, what types of transportation are available when you get there, what customs you would be expected to observe, what language or languages are spoken, what type of clothing is worn, what medical treatment would be needed before you went there (vaccinations, etc.), what types of visas or passports would be required, and how much your train/plane/boat/car transportation would cost. Find out about the area's geography, history, politics, religions, agriculture, industry, economy, and shopping. What tourist spots would you visit? What non-tourist spots would you like to see?

Country you will visit _____

Dates of your visit _____

Climate/weather conditions at the time of your visit _____

_____

Geography of the region (primarily mountainous, desert, rainforest, etc.) _____

_____

Main sources of income (agriculture, manufacturing, tourism, etc.) _____

_____

How will you get there and what will it cost? _____

_____

How will you travel when you get there? _____

_____

What type of clothing will you be expected to wear? _____

_____

What languages are spoken there?_____

_____

continue on next page

0-7424-1807-3 Building Grammar & Writing Skills

Name _____ Date _____

Tours in Cyberspace, Continued

What religions are practiced there? _____

_____

What political system governs the country? _____

_____

What customs will you be expected to observe? _____

_____

What vaccinations, etc., should you have before you leave? _____

_____

What passports and visas will be required? _____

_____

What tourist items would you like to buy (rugs, pearls, leather, etc)? _____

_____

Write a short paragraph about your reflections on this research. What did you learn about this country that surprised you? Are you as eager to visit there as you were when you began? How did your views about this country change?

_____

_____

_____

_____

_____

_____

Share your findings with the class. (1) Tell why you chose the country, (2) tell what the country is like, and (3) tell what you learned from doing the research. Use visual aids in your presentation, including maps and pictures.

Name _____ Date _____

Developing an Itinerary

Now that you have learned a great deal about the country you plan to visit, create your two-week itinerary, telling what you would see each day. (Note: If you travel very far, it may take two of your days to get there and another two to return.)

Week 1

Day 1   Leave from_____at _____ o'clock _____(A.M./P.M.)

Arrive at_____at _____ o'clock _____(A.M./P.M.)

Day 2   _____

Day 3   _____

Day 4   _____

Day 5   _____

Day 6   _____

Day 7   _____

Week 2

Day 8   _____

Day 9   _____

Day 10   _____

Day 11   _____

Day 12   _____

Day 13   _____

Day 14   Arrive at_____at _____ o'clock _____(A.M./P.M.)

Create a group travelogue to share with the class. Use pictures, posters, maps, and other visual aids to help classmates understand the unique characteristics of the country you plan to visit. Share your itinerary, showing where you would go and on what days. If you have access to PowerPoint, prepare a PowerPoint slide presentation for the class.

0-7424-1807-3 Building Grammar & Writing Skills

Name _____ Date _____

Refine Until It Shines

Effective revision requires writers to look at their texts from the perspective of a reader, as well as from their own perspectives as writers. As writers read their own writing, they make predictions about the text's progress and evaluate alternative solutions to specific problems. An especially helpful strategy for revising is to set the work aside for a while. Often you will return to your work with a clearer perspective and, often, new and better material. Most writers find it especially helpful to have other people read what they have written. Choose a story you have already written and try to answer the following questions as though you had never read the paper before. Follow this procedure:

1. Read the title. What do you predict the essay will be about on the basis of the title?

_____

2. Read the introductory paragraph. What do you predict the essay will be about?

_____

3. Tell why the intended audience would be interested in knowing this information.

_____

4. Read the body of the essay, including the headings. For each paragraph, tell whether the point you expected was actually developed.

_____   _____

_____   _____

_____   _____

5. Before reading the conclusion, read the title, introduction, and headings again. What conclusion would a reader expect, given what has been said so far?

_____

_____

6. Now, read the original conclusion. Does it meet the expectations set up by the rest of the essay? Why or why not?

_____

_____

Now have someone else read your paper following the same procedure. You will probably find differences in what your reader saw and what you saw. Revise your paper to solve any problems identified by both readings.

83

Name _____ Date _____

Editing and Proofreading

Not all errors are alike, either in their cause or in their effect on readers. Some errors are caused by carelessness or haste; others occur because the writer has not learned a rule. The effect on readers is also different. Some errors can be overlooked by readers as a typo, while others mark a writer as uneducated. For example, if a writer spells *led* as *lead*, the reader might think the error was one of proofreading. On the other hand, if a writer said *he seen* instead of *he saw*, the reader would recognize this as nonstandard English and lose confidence in the writer's ideas. For writers and their ideas to be taken seriously by readers, the writing needs to be as error free as possible, especially when it comes to serious grammatical errors. To rid yourself of careless errors, follow these guidelines:

1. Learn to proofread carefully. This is not an easy task. Because readers tend to skip over words quickly—and the better the reader, the more skipping they do—they find it difficult to slow the reading process enough to find small errors. Proofreading demands that you look at the writing space by space and letter by letter, as well as word by word and sentence by sentence.

2. Read your paper aloud. This forces you to slow down your reading, and you can often hear errors that you don't see.

3. Have someone else read your papers. Professional writers use proofreaders to help them to find errors that they have missed. You, too, can benefit from having another pair of eyes.

For more serious errors, keep a log of your errors so that you have a list of the kinds of problems that recur in your writing. You will probably find that very few rules are the cause of many errors. Once you have identified the causes of the errors, work on one problem at a time.

Using the paper that you read and revised on the previous page, follow steps 1–3 above to edit and proofread. Make a list of errors that you or your reader found. Identify the reason for them as careless errors (*CE*) or errors resulting from rules you didn't know (*Rules*).

Error	**Cause** (*CE or Rules*)
_____	_____
_____	_____
_____	_____
_____	_____
_____	_____
_____	_____

     0-7424-1807-3 Building Grammar & Writing Skills

Name _____ Date _____

Polishing the Visual Appearance

What a piece of writing looks like on a page has a lot to do with how it is read or even *whether* it is read. Below is a Chinese poem written 2000 years ago. Break it into lines to make it more attractive and effective as a poem. Add punctuation as you think best. Remember to capitalize the first word in each line that you create. Add illustrations that reflect the content, and give the poem a title. You may wish to do this on a computer, where you can experiment with different formats and fonts.

> I want to be your friend forever and ever without break or decay
> when the hills are all flat and the rivers are all dry when it lightens
> and thunders in winter when it rains and snows in summer when
> heaven and earth mingle not till then will I part from you.

0-7424-1807-3 Building Grammar & Writing Skills

Name _____ Date _____

Publishing in Portfolios

People in many fields keep portfolios of their best work. Artists, architects, teachers, playwrights, and writers are just a few professionals who develop portfolios of their most successful efforts. A portfolio helps you to grow as a writer by requiring you to make judgments about the quality of your work. It also gives you an opportunity to see that growth and to share, or "publish," your work with an outside audience.

In choosing what to include in your portfolio, you will want to begin by selecting the writing pieces you consider your best. Your teacher will give you specific guidelines about the contents of your portfolio, but here are some of the types of things you may want to consider:

poetry	research papers	responses to literature
short stories	journal entries	reviews of film
essays	reports	art or photography
letters	book reports	reading logs

When you put your portfolio together, you will want to include a table of contents. You will also include a letter introducing the reader to the pieces in the portfolio and explaining why you selected the pieces you did. The portfolio will include these sections, as well as others of your choosing:

Table of contents organized with headings identifying the types of writing pieces, the titles, and the page numbers where they will be found.

Reflective letter describing the contents of your portfolio—what you have included, what you are most proud of, and what you would change if you had more time. You may want to comment on what you learned about the subject matter of the papers, and about yourself as a writer, through this process.

Writing projects including all work that you have decided to showcase as your best writing. Consider as possible choices all assigned writing projects, including writing you have done that was not assigned, such as poetry or stories written on your own. You may even want to include pieces written for other classes.

Visually attractive presentation with portfolio contents assembled in a decorative folder or binder. Design an attractive title page, and create separate pages for each section, with headings telling your readers what will be found in each section.

Reading response from an adult. After you have assembled your portfolio, have an adult relative or adult friend read it and write a response to it. Include the response in a separate section in the portfolio.

Name _____ Date _____

Chronological Sequence

Narrative writing tells a story. The story may contain one event or a sequence of several events. This type of writing includes autobiographies, biographies, short stories, and novels. Even some poems are classified as narrative poems because they, too, tell a story.

Authors write their narratives in chronological, or time, order. Time order dictates that writers recount events as they occurred. Because plot details are related after they have occurred, narratives almost always are written using past tense verbs (dialogue between characters may contain any tense). Words that signify chronological order include *first, second, then, when, next, before, after, finally,* and *during.*

1. Practice time order by placing the following events in chronological order. Number the first event 1, and the last event 12. Using the twelve events, write a brief narrative, including the transition words that designate chronological order. You may add, delete, and change wording to make your narrative more interesting. Don't forget to include time order words.

_____ Anna was invited to a newcomer's party.

_____ Anna moved to a small town.

_____ She neglected to write down the address.

_____ Anna sat on the couch and visited with other women.

_____ She rang the doorbell and was greeted by a woman.

_____ Anna asked, "Is this a newcomers' meeting?"

_____ She drove ten blocks, saw a porch light on, and saw cars parked along the street.

_____ The hostess replied, "No, this is a Kitchen Gadgets party."

_____ She noticed kitchen items for sale on the coffee table.

_____ Anna thought it was tacky to sell things at a newcomers' get-together.

_____ She walked out, drove home, and never did attend a newcomers' meeting.

_____ Anna apologized and excused herself.

2. Think of a conflict between two people. Create a humorous conversation between them. Rewrite the dialogue, creating a serious conversation. Remember to begin a new paragraph each time you change speakers. Choose one of the following pairs of speakers, or better yet, think of one of your own: an 8-year-old brother and a 14-year-old sister, two eighth-grade students writing a poem, two young children playing a game, or two brothers playing catch. Then write a narrative of one or two paragraphs, and place either the humorous or the serious dialogue into the narrative.

87

Name _____ Date _____

Autobiographical Essays

Autobiographies are stories written by writers about themselves. Most cover the writer's entire life and include carefully selected details to give the reader an overall impression of the writer. Readily available excerpts of autobiographies appear in many middle school literature textbooks. Among popular excerpts are selections from Maya Angelou's *I Know Why the Caged Bird Sings* and from Ernesto Galarza's *Barrio Boy*. These selections can be read and enjoyed by themselves or as a preview to the entire autobiography.

Like an excerpt found in an anthology, concentrate on a "slice of your life"—an event that has shaped your life in some specific way. Recall the incident and why you remember it so vividly.

Arrange the narrative events in chronological order on the lines below. Include your reactions to and feelings about each event to the right of the event.

Events	Feelings
_____	_____
_____	_____
_____	_____
_____	_____
_____	_____

How did this experience shape your life? _____

_____

Using anthologized excerpts as models, think about an experience that caused you to behave or believe the way you do. Examples may include why you are always on time, why you always exercise your dog, why you always double check things, or why you can keep a secret. Begin the essay with a startling statement, a question, or a summary statement. Conclude the essay with what you learned from the experience and how you have changed as a result of it. Begin your introductory paragraph here.

_____

_____

_____

_____

_____

88

Name _____ Date _____

Biographical Essays

Biographies recount events of a person's life. But unlike autobiographies, the writers are not writing about themselves. They are writing about someone else's life. Writers of biographies must make every effort to recount only factual information, and they must do so with the utmost accuracy. Dates must be correct, and spelling, especially of names, must be correct. Since biographies highlight significant accomplishments of a person's life, they are almost always complimentary.

Along with the factual details about the person, writers find it helpful to examine the events of the time period in which the subject was alive. Events of the day often influence a person's actions and help to shape their beliefs. For instance, the Great Depression of the 1930s may have caused someone to quit school, or the Civil Rights Movement of the 1960s may have caused someone to give speeches ten years later about equality of women in sports. The combination of the individual's life and the historical events give the reader an overall impression of the subject of the biography.

Interview someone you admire, such as a grandparent, neighbor, or someone who has led a particularly interesting life. Concentrate on a segment of their lives, such as their youth, their teenage years, their years in the armed services, or their first years in the work force. Use the following prewriting guide to get started.

Name of subject _____

Time period covered _____

Where subject lived _____

Highlighted experience _____

_____

Events _____

_____

Before beginning the biographical essay, verify your facts (dates, places, and spelling of names). Write the biographical essay on another sheet of paper. If a scanner is available, scan a picture of the subject taken during the time period covered in your essay and type the paper in a word processing program. Print two copies—one to give to the person whom you interviewed and one to place in a classroom anthology.

0-7424-1807-3 Building Grammar & Writing Skills

Name _____ Date _____

Myths

Myths are ancient stories from a particular culture. Although every land has its own myths, the most commonly recognized myths are Greek, Roman, and Norse. People of these lands created stories over a thousand years ago to explain their world, but their explanations did not stem from scientific principles. Rather they fashioned stories that fall into three main categories: creation myths, explanatory myths, and myths involving heroic adventures. Storytellers then passed on tales such as those of spiders being created (Arachne), of how the seasons came to be (Persephone), and of great adventures of heroes, such as Hercules, Theseus, and Perseus.

Read some Greek, Roman, or Norse myths as models and complete the following activities.

1. Write a myth explaining how or why we have one of the following: ants, snails, rainbows, stars, or clouds. Better yet, write a creation or explanatory myth based on something unique to your geographical area, such as chameleons in Florida, cacti in the Southwest, cranberries in the Northeast, or geodes around the Mississippi River.

2. According to Greek mythology, Poseidon, the god of the sea, became angry and pounded his trident, causing storms at sea. Write an explanatory myth, revealing how a natural phenomenon occurs. Topics may include the length of a day, the seasons, a type of precipitation, or a modern-day event.

3. Create a hero set in modern times who will undertake three adventures (you may wish to divide the narrative into three chapters, one for each adventure). In each adventure, the hero will encounter some conflict or obstacle. Greek heroes often
  • undertake a journey
  • receive help from another (animal, god, goddess, beautiful woman)
  • search for a valuable item
  • figure out a riddle to defeat an adversary successfully
  • possess superhuman abilities

Use the following prewriting guide to organize your narrative.

Name of hero _____   Item sought _____

Adventure #1 _____   Conflict _____

Adventure #2 _____   Conflict _____

Adventure #3 _____   Conflict _____

Help received _____

_____

Riddle _____

_____

Superhuman ability _____

   0-7424-1807-3 Building Grammar & Writing Skills

Name _____ Date _____

The Moral of the Story Is ...

Fables are very short stories containing animal characters. Since fables are so very short, they contain few characters, little description, and little emotion. They always teach a lesson and, therefore, end with a moral. The animals often portray one dominant trait; for instance, owls are wise, foxes are sly, bees are busy, donkeys are stubborn, and peacocks are proud.

1. Read some fables by Aesop as examples. Divide into small groups. Select two or three animals and their dominant traits for your characters. Because your narrative must be short, make certain that every word counts. Type the fable using word processing software. Illustrate the fable. Arrange and paste or tape the fable and the illustrations on poster board. Plan your fable in the space below. Hint: You may wish to think of your moral first.

Characters _____   _____

Events   _____

          _____

          _____

          _____

Dialogue _____

          _____

          _____

          _____

Moral   _____

2. Present your poster to your classmates by reading the fable aloud. One group member could read the narrative and moral sections, one could read the dialogue of the first animal, and one could read the dialogue of the second animal.

3. Place completed displays of the fables around the classroom and vote for the following:

Most creative _____

Most original _____

Best moral _____

 0-7424-1807-3 Building Grammar & Writing Skills

Name _____ Date _____

Short Stories

Short stories are narratives that resemble novels. Like novels they contain character(s), a plot, setting(s), and usually dialogue. The main difference between the short story and the novel is, of course, length. Along with length is complexity; short stories almost always contain less-complicated plots than novels.

To write a short story you will need to think of several elements. Begin by selecting characters for your story. Describe each briefly. What is the relationship among your characters (friends, siblings, strangers, enemies)? One character will be the protagonist, and another character most likely will be the antagonist. Minor characters themselves often do not change, but they may help the major character change.

Protagonist _____

Antagonist _____

Minor character(s) _____

Next select a setting. It may be ordinary, such as a classroom or a mall, or exotic, such as a tropical island or a ski lodge. Regardless of the setting you choose, you must know something about it to describe it accurately.

_____

_____

Now think about conflict. Add a problem for one or more of your characters to face. Problems normally fall into one or more of the following categories: character against another character, character against nature, character struggling with an internal conflict (battling a decision), or character experiencing a fateful event (good or bad luck).

Conflict _____

_____

Normally, the character is not successful right away. The main character usually faces one or more setbacks while trying to resolve the conflict. Think of additional complications that will confront the main character.

Plot complication(s) _____

_____

_____

On another sheet of paper complete a rough draft of your plot sequence. Use a plot sequence chain like the one below to produce a visual of your narrative. Then, write the story as you have begun to develop it.

0-7424-1807-3 Building Grammar & Writing Skills

Name _____ Date _____

Interpreting Poetry

Reading literature is a very active process. Readers create meaning by connecting the words on the page to their own background knowledge and past experiences. Because everyone has had different life experiences, no two people will read a poem or story in exactly the same way. However, because the words remain the same, there will be important similarities in readers' responses. An important first step in reading literature is becoming aware of your own responses. Read the following poem, "To the River." At this point, do not try to determine what it means. Instead, let the words help you recall associations and experiences. As you read, underline or make notes in the margin as the words trigger memories.

To the River

Fair river! In thy bright, clear flow
  Of crystal, wandering water,
Thou art an emblem of the glow
    Of beauty—the unhidden heart—
    The playful maziness of art
In old Alberto's daughter;

But when within thy wave she looks—
    Which glistens then, and trembles—
Why, then, the prettiest of brooks
    Her worshipper resembles;
For in my heart, as in thy stream,
    Her image deeply lies—
His heart which trembles at the beam
    Of her soul-searching eyes.

1. What associations and memories with rivers does the poem cause you to recall? Does this poem remind you of somewhere you have been? Another poem or story you have read? A movie you have seen? Briefly describe what is called to mind.

   _____

   _____

   _____

   _____

2. What images stand out? On a separate sheet of paper, sketch a picture capturing some image from the poem.

continue on next page

0-7424-1807-3 Building Grammar & Writing Skills

Name _____ Date _____

Interpreting Poetry, Continued

3. What do you see happening in the poem? Describe it briefly.

_____

_____

_____

_____

4. If you had to select one important word in the poem, what would it be? Why would you choose that word?

_____

_____

5. Choose a reading partner and compare responses to questions 3 and 4. What similarities and differences do you find among the responses? After you have discussed these responses with your reading partner, discuss them with the entire class.

Similarities _____

_____

Differences _____

_____

6. You probably found that you revised your interpretation somewhat as a result of the discussions. Write a short paragraph telling (a) how you first reacted to the poem and (b) how your reading of the poem changed.

_____

_____

_____

_____

_____

_____

7. "To the River" is from Edgar Allan Poe's collection of *Poems from Youth*. How would knowing the author influence your reading of the poem?

_____

Name _____ Date _____

Short Fiction: Chinese Fables

Below are two Chinese fables, each offering some comment about human behavior. First, try to predict what you think the fable will be about from reading the title. After reading it, state briefly what message or theme statement you think it offers. Tell briefly of some personal experience that you associate with the story.

Suspicion
by Li Zi

A man who lost his axe suspected his neighbor's son of stealing it. He watched the way the lad walked exactly like a thief. He watched the boy's expression—it was that of a thief. He watched the way he talked—just like a thief. In short, all his gestures and actions proclaimed him guilty of theft. But later he found his axe himself when he went out to dig. After that, when he saw his neighbor's son, all the lad's gestures and actions looked quite unlike those of a thief.

Theme Statement _____

_____

Personal Experience _____

_____

Short Sightedness
A joke of the 19th century by an unknown author

Two men were short-sighted, but instead of admitting it, both of them boasted of keen vision. One day they heard that a tablet was to be hung in a temple. So each of them found out what was written on it beforehand. When the day came, they both went to the temple. Looking up, one said, "Look, aren't the characters 'Brightness and Uprighteousness'?" "And the smaller ones. There! You can't see them, they say, 'Written by so and so in a certain month, on a certain day'!" said the other. A passerby asked what they were looking at. When told, the man laughed. "The tablet hasn't been hoisted up, so how can you see the characters?" he asked.

Theme Statement _____

_____

Personal Experience _____

_____

Write your own original fable, and give it a title that suggests the meaning.
Read your fable to the class.

95

   0-7424-1807-3 Building Grammar & Writing Skills

Name _____ Date _____

Visual Images: The Novel

Much of the meaning in what we read comes to us in visual images. Below is a passage from "Winter Memories," in Chapter III of Willa Cather's novel *O Pioneers*, describing her recollections of winter on the Nebraska prairie.

> Winter has settled down over the Divide again; the season in which Nature recuperates, in which she sinks to sleep between the fruitfulness of autumn and the passion of spring. The birds have gone. The teeming life that goes on down in the long grass is exterminated. The prairie dog keeps his hole. The rabbits run shivering from one frozen garden patch to another and are hard put to find frostbitten cabbage stalks. At night the coyotes roam the wintry waste, howling for food. The variegated fields are all one color now; the pastures, the stubble, the roads, the sky are the same leaden gray. The hedgerows and trees are scarcely perceptible against the bare earth, whose slaty hue they have taken on. The ground is frozen so hard that it bruises the foot to walk in the roads or in the ploughed fields. It is like an iron country, and the spirit is oppressed by its rigor and melancholy. One could easily believe that in that dead landscape the germs of life and fruitfulness were extinct forever.

On another sheet of paper, draw some image from the landscape that you see in this passage.

1. List three images in Cather's word picture that suggest winter's harsh desolation.

_____   _____   _____

2. List four animals. _____

3. List four types of vegetation. _____

4. Choose a word or phrase from the passage that could be substituted for the title "Winter Memories"—something that you think gives a strong suggestion of what the season was like and how Cather felt about it. Explain your choice. Share responses with the class.

Word or Phrase _____

_____

_____

5. Like Cather, write a passage describing your own strong recollections of winter or some other season, using vivid examples and word pictures. Draw an illustration to accompany your word picture. Share your description and picture with the class.

0-7424-1807-3 Building Grammar & Writing Skills

Name _____ Date _____

Formal Responses to Literature

The following student essay was written about Alice Walker's short story, "Everyday Use." The assignment was to read the story, and then write a response that included answers to these questions:

- What happens in the story?
- What point do you think the author is making in the story?
- Do you think the story mirrors real life?

Read the essay, and try to determine how well the student completed the assignment. (The paragraphs are numbered to help you answer questions at the end of the essay.)

Everyday Dreams, by Andrea Guyon

(1) Television series often have episodes in which characters are granted wishes. The characters carefully select the wishes that they think will satisfy their fondest desires. Characteristically, no matter how much thought is put into the wishes, the characters are unable to live with the consequences. Like many people who have dreams and wishes, Mrs. Johnson and her daughter Dee, in Alice Walker's "Everyday Use," envision worlds that hold the promise of wonderful lives. However, these dreams do not reflect their real desires. What Dee and her mother really value–in sharp contrast to their dreams–is the lives they already lead: their "everyday lives."

(2) Mrs. Johnson's dream centers on fame and success for herself and her family. She imagines herself as a grand lady appearing on the Johnny Carson show. The world would see her "the way that [her] daughter would want [her] to be" (Walker 932). She fondly reflects on the praise she would receive for raising such a fine girl. Dee's success in the outside world would, of course, be Mrs. Johnson's own accomplishment. But when Dee comes home, Mrs. Johnson is unable to accept the daughter that she has envisioned. She sees that Dee's interest in her heritage is as superficial as the trendy clothes she wears. Dee's grand style, Mrs. Johnson recognizes, does not "fit" in the real world of plain, black folk. More important, she sees the shallowness in Dee's values.

(3) Much like her mother, Dee creates her own fantasy world. She attempts to get in touch with her roots by coming home and seeking heirloom pieces. What she fails to realize is that her roots are most evident in the lives of her immediate family, whom she disdains. She feels that she must take an original African name–Wangero–to show her heritage. Being named after several generations of women in her family is not heritage enough for her. In attempting to create her dream, Dee has rejected the very life she once lived. When she lived at her mother's house, she had sat on the benches made by her father and used the butter churn Uncle Buddy had whittled out of a tree in the yard. Now she sees the churn and bench simply as symbols of her imagined heritage to put on display. Although she insists that she loves these artifacts, almost in the same breath she tells her mother and her sister Maggie that they need to cast off their old-fashioned ways. She tells Maggie, "It's really a new day for us. But from the way you and Mama still live, you'd never know it."

(4) Walker uses Maggie, the disfigured sister, as a foil character, showing the contrast between Mrs. Johnson's and Dee's inability to appreciate the real world and Maggie's acceptance of her life as it is. Maggie has created a realistic and satisfying life for herself. She does not see family artifacts as pieces of her heritage; she sees them as part of her daily life. She makes her dream world out of the life she has. Dee tells her that she "ought to try to make something of [herself]." Maggie *will* make something of herself by marrying John Thomas and living a simple life. Unlike Dee, Maggie holds within her the heritage that Dee only imagines: "[I can] remember…without the quilts," she says.

(5) Although Dee continues with her shallow, trendy life, Mrs. Johnson comes to acknowledge and share Maggie's values. Maggie already knew, and Mrs. Johnson learns, that real life is what they value most. Everyday life is better than a dream.

97

Name _____ Date _____

Formal Responses to Literature, Continued

1. Tell briefly what you think happens in the story, based on what the student writer has said in each paragraph, beginning with paragraph 2.

Paragraph 2 _____

_____

Paragraph 3 _____

_____

Paragraph 4 _____

_____

Paragraph 5 _____

_____

2. According to the student writer, what point does the author, Alice Walker, make? Find lines in paragraphs 1 and 5 that make the point.

Paragraph 1 _____

_____

Paragraph 5 _____

_____

3. Does the student writer think the story mirrors real life? Explain, giving paragraph numbers.

_____

_____

Choose a short story to read. Using the student writer's essay as a model, write a formal response to your story, answering these questions: What happens in the story? What point do you think the author is making in the story? Do you think the story mirrors real life?

_____

_____

_____

98

Name _____ Date _____

Persuasive Techniques

One type of composition that you will often need to write is one that uses persuasion. It may be a letter to a friend, newspaper, or school official; it may be an oral presentation in a meeting; it may be a state test or an entrance exam to get into college; or it may be an on-the-job report. In all instances the intention remains the same: to convince someone that your view on an issue is clear and worth consideration. An effective format for persuasion is one that gives the opposing argument before giving your own. This way, your readers know that you are knowledgeable about the subject, since you have studied both sides. The student essay below uses this four-part organization: (1) introduction stating the facts of the case, (2) summary of the opposing arguments, (3) presentation of the student's arguments, and (4) conclusion, telling why the student's position is better than the opposition's. Read the essay and answer the questions on the following page.

Making Advertisers Responsible with Child-Targeted Advertisements

Today, many manufacturers target children in their advertisements because they know that children influence parents' decisions to buy. Sometimes the products are harmless or even educational. However, cereal and toys make up the majority of advertising to children, and often these foods are not healthful and the toys are not safe. The goal of these companies is to make a profit. However, it is unethical to focus on children, who are likely to believe all the promises they hear in a commercial, and the advertising industry needs to set up strict guidelines about advertising for children.

Spokespeople for the advertising industry argue that advertising is not necessarily harmful to children. They say that parents need to teach children from an early age about the difference between programs and advertisements. They also argue that schools should be teaching about advertising messages and persuasion techniques to make children better consumers. Some advertisers say that children would want to buy the products even if they didn't see the commercials. They also point out that most companies are responsible about their advertisements to children, and no regulation is necessary.

However, advertisers are clearly ignoring all kinds of evidence that advertising to children is harmful because they want to continue making big profits. In an ordinary week, children often watch as much as 25 to 30 hours of television. Saturday morning and after school are especially big times for television viewing by children. This brings in big dollars to the companies selling the products. Because parents are busy and cannot monitor every minute of their children's viewing time, they often do not know what kinds of commercials children are seeing. If the programs are in good taste, they assume that the advertisements are also appropriate. Advertisers use music, singing, dancing, famous people, other children, and animation to make children believe that a product will be good for them. Because the children often do not see the difference between programs and advertisements, these ads cause children to form positive attitudes toward the products being advertised, and they pressure their parents to buy them.

Advertisers need to become responsible in their advertising to children and monitor the advertisements on children's programming. Instead of putting the blame on parents and schools, they need to provide useful information about the quality of a product. They should aim their messages to the parents, who can make wise decisions about the product. If advertisers become responsible, they will be doing themselves a favor as well as the consumers. Parents will form positive attitudes toward the products and be more likely to buy them.

0-7424-1807-3 Building Grammar & Writing Skills

Name _____ Date _____

Analyzing Persuasive Techniques

As with all writing, persuasive compositions require close attention to audience and purpose. You need to know what the audience already knows and what their interests are. You need to know whether to use formal or informal language. You need to decide whether emotional or logical appeals would be more effective. And you need to convince your audience that you are knowledgeable and trustworthy. On the lines 1–4 below, briefly summarize each paragraph in the student essay on page 99. Then answer questions 5–11 about audience, purpose, and the writer's role. Discuss answers with classmates.

1. Introduction (states the facts of the case)

_____

_____

2. Summary of the opposing arguments (Write on the back if you need more space.)

_____

_____

3. Presentation of the writer's arguments (Write on the back if you need more space.)

_____

_____

4. Conclusion (tells readers why the writer's position is better than that of the opposition)

_____

_____

5. What is the writer's purpose? _____

6. Who are appropriate audiences? _____

_____

7. Why would these audiences be interested? _____

_____

8. Is the language formal or informal in this essay? _____

9. Why is it appropriate for the audience? _____

10. Does the writer use emotional appeals, logical appeals, or both? _____

11. Does the writer appear knowledgeable and trustworthy about the topic? _____

0-7424-1807-3 Building Grammar & Writing Skills

Name _____ Date _____

Planning a Persuasive Essay

Now plan your own persuasive essay following the four-part format. Imagine that your school plans to merge with a slightly larger, nearby school that was once your school's rival in sports. Take a position either for or against the merger. Provide an introduction, a summary of the opposing argument, presentation of your arguments, and a conclusion. Your audience is voters in the school district. Your views will be published in a special school section in the local news paper. Instead of actually writing out the whole essay, just list the ideas that you would use if you were to write it.

1. Introduction _____

_____

_____

_____

2. Summary of the opposing view _____

_____

_____

_____

_____

_____

3. Presentation of your arguments _____

_____

_____

_____

_____

_____

_____

4. Conclusion _____

_____

_____

_____

 0-7424-1807-3 Building Grammar & Writing Skills

Name _____ Date _____

Are You Persuaded?

Frequently, the catalyst for a piece of persuasive writing is something someone else has written. All major newspapers and magazines have "Letters to the Editor" sections, containing readers' responses to some issue under discussion. They may support or challenge the publication's position, or they may respond to another reader's comments. Customarily, these letters begin by stating what the publication said before making their own point. Try your hand at responding to someone else's ideas by writing about one of Thomas Jefferson's "rules" for living a successful life, listed below. Write a short persuasive essay telling what Jefferson said, whether you agree or disagree, and why. Explain your answer with evidence from your personal experiences, from other reading, or from your observations of life.

1. Never put off until tomorrow what you can do today.
2. Never trouble another for what you can do yourself.
3. Never spend your money before you have it.
4. Never buy what you do not want because it is cheap; it will be dear to you.
5. Pride costs us more than hunger, thirst, and cold.

What Jefferson said _____

_____

_____

_____

Do you agree or disagree? Why? _____

_____

_____

_____

_____

_____

_____

_____

_____

_____

　　0-7424-1807-3 Building Grammar & Writing Skills

Name _____ Date _____

Using Research Analysis

Longer persuasive essays often result from a writer's analysis of something that has happened in the media or in the culture at large. Below are three topics related to public issues. Choose one to write about in a one- or two-page persuasive paper. To complete this assignment
- Do the research described.
- Decide what you think about what you find.
- Write an introduction pointing out the issue and its importance.
- Describe what you learned.
- Tell what you think about what you learned.
- Conclude by telling why this information is important.

1. Write a persuasive paper in which you analyze a current ad campaign, clothing style, television series, or politician. Your audience for this paper is members of the class. Pretend that you are a reporter presenting the kinds of descriptions and details that will make your listeners clearly picture the person or issue. Base your description on your first-hand observation-watching the movie/TV program, reporting observations from the street, reading, etc.

2. Write a paper in which you fully characterize a current famous person or group, either someone you find ridiculous or someone you greatly admire. Your audience is readers of your school newspaper. Keep in mind that your readers (students, teachers, administration) may not agree with you, or they may not be as familiar with this person as you are. After describing this person and offering your personal views, add some analysis to your paper by commenting on what the fame of this person says about the culture. What are the implications of people like this having influence in the world?

3. Identify a current public issue about which you have an opinion. You may need to browse newspapers, news programs, etc. Editorials and "Letters to the Editor" sections are good starting places. Pretend that you are applying to attend a particular school and have been asked to send a persuasive writing sample to the admissions counselor. This audience will value arguments with reasoned support and analysis.

After you have written the paper to the specified audience, present your argument orally to the class, inviting feedback and discussion about the following:
- Clarity of your ideas
- Accuracy of your observations
- Appropriateness of your language and ideas for the specified audience
- Strength of your argument (were they persuaded?)

0-7424-1807-3 Building Grammar & Writing Skills

Name _____ Date _____

Taking Standardized Tests

Competency tests given in schools at various grades or college admission tests given to incoming students often call for a persuasive essay. Normally these writing tests are timed (usually 45–60 minutes) and they ask students to write on a specific topic. They may suggest an audience, although they may not. They also commonly provide a format to follow, very often a five-paragraph theme, in which you state your topic in the introduction, provide three supporting evidence paragraphs, and conclude the essay in a final paragraph. Notice that the essay on advertising on page 99 fits this format if you take out the opposing argument (paragraph 2) and break the writer's argument (paragraph 3) into three separate paragraphs. Here is how that essay would look as a five-paragraph theme.

Making Advertisers Responsible with Child-Targeted Advertisements

Today, many manufacturers target children in their advertisements because they know that children influence parents' decisions to buy. Sometimes the products are harmless or even educational. However, cereal and toys make up the majority of advertising to children, and often these foods are not healthful and the toys are not safe. The goal of these companies is to make a profit. However, it is unethical to focus on children, who are likely to believe all the promises they hear in a commercial, and the advertising industry needs to set up strict guidelines about advertising for children.

Advertisers are clearly ignoring all kinds of evidence that advertising to children is harmful because they want to continue making big profits. In an ordinary week, children often watch as much as 25 to 30 hours of television. Saturday morning and after school are especially big times for television viewing by children. This brings in big dollars to the companies selling the products.

Because parents are busy and cannot monitor every minute of their children's viewing time, they often do not know what kinds of commercials children are seeing. If the programs are in good taste, they assume that the advertisements are also appropriate.

Advertisers use music, singing, dancing, famous people, other children, and animation to make children believe that a product will be good for them. Because the children often do not see the difference between programs and advertisements, these ads cause children to form positive attitudes toward the products being advertised, and they pressure their parents to buy them.

Advertisers need to become responsible in their advertising to children. Instead of putting the blame on parents and schools, they need to stop using techniques that do not provide useful information about the quality of a product. They should aim their messages to the parents, who can make wise decisions about the product. If advertisers become responsible, they will be doing themselves a favor as well as the consumers. Parents will form positive attitudes toward the products and be more likely to buy them.

Using the format above, write an essay of 200–300 words on one of the topics listed below or another topic of your choice. You may want to time yourself in writing this essay to simulate a real test situation. Correct grammar, spelling, sentence structure, and punctuation are important.

• Our school should (or should not) merge with the rival school. (Use plan from page 101.)
• Schools should (or should not) provide soy burgers rather than hamburgers in cafeterias.
• Some type of community service should (or should not) be required of all students.

Name _____ Date _____

Investigate, Corroborate, Relate

Research reports require writers to obtain information from other sources. To complete a research assignment, you will have to read extensively about your topic in secondary sources, take notes, organize information, and present the information in a well-written paper. In some instances you may also conduct your own investigation by interviewing or surveying primary sources. Because there are so many steps, research papers take more time to write than other school papers. However, because of their in-depth nature, they are often more exciting, interesting, and rewarding than shorter projects.

Selecting a Topic. When completing a research project you should find a topic that interests you, since you will be conducting in-depth research over a period of several weeks. A good way to begin is to brainstorm several possible topics.

Think of the type of work you would like to do in the future. This career may require training beyond high school or may require college or technical education. To help you decide, you may wish to question relatives, neighbors, and parents about their careers. List three possible careers below:

_____

_____

_____

Select one of the above careers. You may need to limit the topic before you continue. For instance, if you wrote *doctor* as one of your potential topics, you will want to narrow the focus to a specific type (pediatrician, internist, oncologist, ophthalmologist, or podiatrist). If you wrote *teacher*, you will want to designate an age level and possibly a specific area of instruction, such as social sciences, mathematics, or foreign language.

Name your limited topic career choice _____

Why does this career interest you? _____

_____

_____

_____

_____

 0-7424-1807-3 Building Grammar & Writing Skills

Name _____ Date _____

Compile Source Cards

As you begin this research project, you will need to gather possible sources to read. For each source you select, determine whether it will be helpful before you invest too much time reading it. As you examine your sources, look at the following: copyright date, extent and depth of information, and readability level. Sources that do not contain the information you need or that are too difficult to read will not help you achieve your goal. When writing most papers, such as one about careers, current information is essential. Therefore, you will want to concentrate on most recently published sources.

When you write the body of the paper, you will need to know from which source you obtained your information. One way to keep track of the sources you have consulted is source cards. For each source, complete a separate card with the following information:

  1. A number in the upper left-hand corner of each card, with a different number for each source card
  2. The call number (if the source has one) or Web address (URL) in the lower left-hand corner
  3. The bibliographic citation (author, title, and publication information)

Fill in the information for one of the sources you have gathered. You will not need to fill in all the blanks.

Name of author(s) _____

Date of publication _____

Title of article _____

Title of book, magazine, or newspaper _____

Publisher (book) _____

Place of publication _____

Volume number (magazine) _____ Section letter (newspaper) _____

Page numbers used _____

Internet URL _____

Date accessed _____

Brief description of contents _____

_____

Use this form as a model as you fill out your source cards for books, magazines, newspapers, and Internet sites.

0-7424-1807-3 Building Grammar & Writing Skills

Name _____ Date _____

Take Notes from Secondary Sources

As you read about your chosen career, you will find that information falls into several categories. These categories include

- Background information about the nature of the job
- On-the-job working conditions
- Education and/or training needed
- Salary and benefits (health care, pension)
- Advancement opportunities
- Future outlook for the profession

Take notes on the above information, keeping the following in mind:

1. Write notes on 3" x 5" index cards. Use a separate card for each note.

2. Write the number from the upper-left hand corner of the source card on the note card. This reference code number is a great time-saver; it frees you from writing the title of the source or the name of the author(s) each time you write a new note card. Of course, you may write the title and/or author each time if you choose.

3. In the upper right-hand corner, label each note card with the category or heading that the notation supports.

4. Use plenty of note cards—do not mix topics or sources on one card.

Examine the sample note cards and answer the questions that follow.

#2 Working Conditions	#4 Outlook
"Dental assistants work in comfortable surroundings. Their office environment is climate controlled and antiseptic." page 309	The need for dental assistants is expected to increase more than average in the next ten years. page 101

When taking notes, you may either paraphrase information, or you may copy the information word for word. When you copy word for word, be certain to place quotation marks around the copied sentences.

  1. Write the first four words of the note card that has been copied word for word.

    _____

  2. From what page was it copied? _____   **3.** What is the source number? _____

  4. Write the category of the note card that contains a paraphrase _____

  5. From what page was it copied? _____   **6.** What is the source number? _____

After you complete your note cards, organize them into piles, one pile for each category. Then arrange the cards in the order the information will appear in the paper. You will use these later when you complete a working outline.

     0-7424-1807-3 Building Grammar & Writing Skills

Name _____ Date _____

Gather Information from Primary Sources

If you want to add original research about the career you have examined, you may want to conduct a survey or an interview. For example, if you are interested in becoming an automotive mechanic and can find three mechanics, you may ask each one to fill out a survey. If you know only one automotive mechanic, an interview asking the mechanic what the job is like would be helpful.

1. Using the following as a model, design a survey to collect data. Be certain to give the respondent specific instructions concerning how to fill out the survey.

Please complete the following survey using the 1–5 scale to express your opinion about your career. Circle the number that best fits your feelings:

1 = extremely low   2 = low   3 = average   4 = above average   5 = very high

Job satisfaction	1	2	3	4	5
Amount of schooling needed	1	2	3	4	5
Variety of tasks	1	2	3	4	5
Amount of stress	1	2	3	4	5
Interest level	1	2	3	4	5
Flexibility in hours	1	2	3	4	5
Salary and benefits	1	2	3	4	5
Advancement opportunities	1	2	3	4	5

2. Interview one or more people in the field, either in person or by telephone. Prepare your interview questions ahead of time and refrain from asking personal information. For instance, rather than asking how much a person makes, you could ask for a salary range for beginning workers in the field. On another sheet of paper, write the questions you will ask. Questions that encourage lengthier responses work best; it is a good idea to avoid questions that can be answered with a *yes* or *no*.

Sample Questions
1. How did you become interested in this career?
2. What is the most rewarding aspect of your job?
3. If you could change one aspect about your job, what would it be?

You will want to create a source card and note cards for each primary source. A sample source card and note card follow.

#6
Hanks, Paul. Personal Interview.
January 23, 2003

#6   Salary
Salaries for beginning newspaper reporters range from $19,000 to $22,000 a year in the Midwest. They are greater in the East and West.

0-7424-1807-3 Building Grammar & Writing Skills

Name _____ Date _____

Create a Working Outline

A working outline helps you to stay focused and organized while writing your paper. Each major heading appears next to the Roman numerals. Write subheadings next to the capital letters. If you wish to include details under the subheadings, write them after Arabic numerals (write these on another sheet of paper and indicate where the detail belongs—I. A. 1., for example). Remember that working outlines may be changed as you write the research paper.

_____
Working Title

I. Nature of the Job
   A. _____
   B. _____
   C. _____

II. Working Conditions
   A. _____
   B. _____
   C. _____

III. Education and Training
   A. _____
   B. _____
   C. _____

IV. Salary and Benefits
   A. _____
   B. _____
   C. _____

V. Advancement Opportunities
   A. _____
   B. _____
   C. _____

VI. Future Outlook for the Profession
   A. _____
   B. _____
   C. _____

0-7424-1807-3 Building Grammar & Writing Skills

Name _____ Date _____

Format the Paper

From the outline on the previous page, you can see the parts of the body of the research paper. Below is a visual representation of what the finished project will look like.

Title of Paper

First and Last Name
Name of Teacher
Date

Title Page

Title of Paper

Introduction: Includes the thesis sentence, which previews sections in the body of the paper.

Nature of the Job

First sentence in your own words followed by research. Include quotations and paraphrases.

1

Page One

Future Outlook

Topic sentence and information concerning the outlook for those who currently work in this field.

Conclusions

Summary of findings and statement about whether you are still interested in pursuing this career.

5

Last Page of Body

Works Cited

First entry (alphabetized with hanging indentation)

Second entry (with hanging Indentation)

Third entry, etc.

Fourth entry—use an entry for each source quoted or para-phrased in the paper.

6

Citations Page

Refer to this page as you write your paper.

110

Name _____ Date _____

Write the Paper

Writing the paper will involve reporting what you have read. Once you have taken notes and have created a working outline, you are ready to begin writing the body of the paper. As with any paper, you will begin with an introduction, include a detailed body, and end with a conclusion. The introduction and conclusion will contain mostly your own words.

The body will contain your ideas and the information from your note cards. Since the body of the paper comprises most of the paper, it is important to gracefully integrate your own ideas and words with those of your sources. Usually you will begin each section and each paragraph with your own statement(s), followed by source information and occasional comments of your own. In other words, you will make a point and support it with various sources. You will make an even stronger case if you can support your statements with more than one source.

Read the following excerpt from a student's research paper. Write the student's words on the first lines and the source information from each of the three sources. The introductory tags will help you recognize information from the sources.

> Thirty years ago the term "Webmaster" did not exist. Today, because of growth of the Internet, the term Webmaster has become commonplace. According to *Technology Occupations*, Webmasters oversee "every aspect of a Web site. They study issues such as accessibility and approve information that appears on the site" (62). Webmaster Tara Lowman agrees, stating that according to her experience, Webmasters place a high priority on accessibility for clients since time is so very important in the workplace (287). Concerning site content, David Short says, "Webmasters do not actually create content for the Web site but approve or reject the information and design that has been already created" (71).

Student's Words _____

_____

_____

Source Information #1 _____

    Quotation or Paraphrase? _____

Source Information #2 _____

    Quotation or Paraphrase? _____

Source Information #3 _____

    Quotation or Paraphrase? _____

Calculate the percentage of the student's words compared to the percentage from sources. Your research paper will approximate this same percentage.

Name _____ Date _____

Identify Sources

There are two ways to identify information that you have borrowed from other sources. One is the use of introductory tags. The other is the use of parenthetical citations.

Introductory tags, such as *says, states, suggests, agrees, explains, describes, illustrates, points out, reports, emphasizes,* and *according to,* along with the source's name, title, or other identifying information, signal to the reader that borrowed information follows. Words such as *believes* should be avoided since you, as the researcher/writer, know only what the source has actually stated.

Read the following excerpt from a student's research paper. Then list the sources in the excerpt and the introductory tags used to identify them.

> In addition to salary, pension and health packages are important when considering a job. Edward Kinman, a career counselor, says, "Very often students are lured by a slightly higher salary without health or retirement benefits because they do not understand that on average these benefits comprise roughly 25% of a salary package. Therefore, a person whose gross salary is $30,000 is actually making $37,500 with benefits." According to Dennis Gomez, too often students can be talked into taking the job described by Kinman for $32,000 gross salary with no benefits, losing $5,500 a year in critical benefits. Robert Watson, president of Career Placement, Inc., agrees, saying, "Young people have no concept of how important health insurance and pension plans are."

Sources	**Introductory Tags**
_____	_____
_____	_____
_____	_____

As you write the body of your research paper, begin each section with your own statement(s) supported by quotations and paraphrases of source information. Use tags to introduce sources; add page numbers, when given, after both quotations and paraphrases.

On the lines below begin writing a section of your paper, following the above guidelines. Circle or highlight all introductory tags.

_____

_____

_____

_____

Name _____ Date _____

Give Credit Where Credit Is Due

In addition to letting readers know what information comes from sources, writers also must let readers know where the full text of the source information can be found. With this information readers have the option to read the complete source. A Works Cited page at the end of the research paper provides readers with an alphabetically arranged list of all the sources quoted or paraphrased in the paper. The reader can locate the correct source on the Works Cited page from information in the introductory tag and the parenthetical citations (information in parentheses following the borrowed information). Parenthetical citations follow these guidelines:

- If the author's name is used to introduce the source information, the writer puts only the page number(s) in parentheses. This is the most frequent type of parenthetical citation.
- If the author's name is not used to introduce the borrowed information, the writer puts the author's name and page number in parentheses.
- If the author's name is not known, the article title and page number are in parentheses.

The following information is from a student paper. By looking at the introductory tag and the parenthetical information, you can find the entry on the Works Cited page. On the lines below, copy the full source information from the bibliographic entries located at the bottom of this page.

Jerome Artman, copyeditor for the *Sunnydale Journal*, reports that many copyeditors work in their own homes and set their own hours. Although there appears to be much flexibility concerning hours, strict deadlines must be met ("The Job Center: Focus on Careers as a Copyeditor" J5).

_____

_____

According to Annette Cunningham, "Copyeditors pay attention to detail, reading and correcting errors in grammar, capitalization, and punctuation. Often in-house style sheets dictate certain rules and formats; copyeditors make certain these rules are followed" (28).

_____

_____

Bibliographic Entries

Cunningham, Annette. *Writing Careers*. Chicago: Wright Press, 2000.

"The Job Center: Focus on Careers as a Copyeditor." *Sunnydale Journal* 9 May 1998: J5.

0-7424-1807-3 Building Grammar & Writing Skills

Name _____ Date _____

Create a Works Cited Page

When writing a research paper in language arts, you will most likely be instructed to use MLA style. That means your bibliographic list of the works you used follows the format established by the Modern Language Association, which is often called MLA for short. A complete discussion of how to list sources appears in the *MLA Handbook for Writers of Research Papers*.

When completing your Works Cited page, follow these guidelines.

1. Capitalize and center the page heading, Works Cited.

2. Arrange your source cards in alphabetical order by the authors' last names. If a source has no author listed, use the first word of the title, disregarding *a, an,* and *the*. Do not order the cards by the number you used when you found the sources and wrote your source cards.

3. Copy the information on the source cards using correct bibliographic citations. The list of works should be presented with hanging indentation (see examples below and page 110). Hanging indentation helps your reader to readily focus on authors' last names.

4. Double space your entries.

5. Include only the sources that you actually quoted or paraphrased in your paper.

Sample Entries

Baker, Stan. "Physicians and Surgeons in Rural Areas." *Daily News 7* November 2002: B3.

Krannich, Ronald L., and Caryl Rae Krannich. "Physicians." *The Best Jobs for the 21st Century.* 3rd ed. Manassas Park, Virginia: Impact Publications, Inc., 1998. 158–59.

"Surgeons." *Careers in Focus: Physicians.* Chicago: Ferguson, 2000. 175–79.

On another sheet of paper, practice writing the sample entries below by putting the information into correct MLA form. Alphabetize the list.

1. A book called *Careers Without College: Makeup Artist* by Kathryn A. Quinlan, which was published in Mankato, Minnesota, by Capstone Books in 1999

2. An article titled, "More Than a Pill Counter" by Kevin Woodward, which appeared on page 7 in section A of the September 26, 2002, newspaper called the *Quincy Herald-Whig*

3. A chapter titled, "Wildlife Management," which appears in the book *Cool Careers for Girls with Animals* by Ceel Pasternak and Linda Thornburg from page 49 through 56; published in 1999 in Manassas Park, Virginia, by Impact Publications, Inc.

114

Name _____ Date _____

Put the Paper Together

Reread your research paper carefully and complete the following checklist before handing it in to your teacher. Refer to page 110 for proper formatting.

_____ Title page: Title centered one third down the page; first and last name of student, name of teacher, and date two-thirds down the page, single spaced

_____ All other pages: One-inch page margins; double-spaced text throughout; subheadings in bold type; each page number centered at the bottom of the page

_____ Page 1: Title centered and bold; introduction—in own words—includes thesis sentence, which previews the six sections that the body of the paper will discuss

Check each paragraph in the body to see that you have introduced the paragraph with a topic statement of your own (not part of the source material) and that each paragraph sticks to a single topic. Use as many blanks as apply.

Paragraph	Main Idea of Paragraph	Topic Sentence Student-Written?	Paragraph Sticks to One Topic?
#1	_____	_____	_____
#2	_____	_____	_____
#3	_____	_____	_____
#4	_____	_____	_____
#5	_____	_____	_____
#6	_____	_____	_____
#7	_____	_____	_____
#8	_____	_____	_____
#9	_____	_____	_____
#10	_____	_____	_____

_____ Conclusion: Summarize research in your own words; include whether you are still interested in pursuing this career.

_____ Works Cited: Entries in alphabetical order, hanging indentation, double-spaced, MLA order of information; titles of books and periodicals italicized; titles of articles and chapters in quotation marks; all sources quoted or paraphrased in the paper are listed.

0-7424-1807-3 Building Grammar & Writing Skills

Name _____ Date _____

Peer Review Form

Before handing in your paper, it is a good idea to have someone else read it. Ask a peer to read your paper. In the space provided for each section below, have your peer editor list the page number and words or phrases containing errors in Standard English. The peer editor should refrain from writing on your report.

Peer Editor's Name _____

1. Are all words spelled correctly? If not, list the page number and the incorrect word(s).

_____

_____

2. Is standard punctuation used? List deviations from standard rules.

_____

_____

3. Is standard capitalization used? List deviations from standard rules. _____

_____

_____

4. Are sentences grammatically correct? List suggested corrections. _____

_____

_____

5. Does the paper contain any awkward sentences? List suggested corrections. _____

_____

_____

6. Are there places where different word choice would clarify the meaning or the idea of the passage? List those places. _____

_____

_____

7. Are there any questions left unanswered in this report? If so, what are they? _____

_____

_____

8. What is the most interesting part of this report?

_____

_____

0-7424-1807-3 Building Grammar & Writing Skills

Name _____ Date _____

General Guidelines

In contrast to writing you do for friends or family, business and technical writing requires you to be particular about following standard rules of English and a particular format. Writing for work allows no margin for error. Employers and customers are not tolerant of writers with unclear ideas, careless page appearance, or misspellings. Advertisements, business letters, e-mail, reports, and even business cards must all convey a public image that reflects high standards. In this section, you will create documents for seeking a job, as well as those that you may be asked to prepare once you have a position. Below are five important guidelines for writing effective technical documents. Answer the questions under each by circling all that apply. Discuss your choices with classmates.

1. Know your audience, and always write with that reader in mind.

Which of the following would most likely be the audience for technical documents?

minister	neighbor	best friend	principal
4H Club	sales clerk	librarian	school board

2. Know your purpose, state it at the beginning, and stick to it.

Which of the following would be likely purposes for a technical document?

to explain a process   to report results

to ask for help   to entertain an audience

3. Use a clear and predictable organizational plan in presenting your information.

Which of the following organizational plans seem the most appropriate?

mystery with surprise ending   order of importance

flashback   chronological sequence

4. Design a professional appearance with headings, graphics, and white space.

Which of the following headings is the most appropriate and informative for a report on dress codes for a particular company?

Let's Get with It!

Guidelines for Professional Appearance

Report from the Director

5. Proofread for clarity and accuracy. Proofread again. Have two other people proofread.

Find and correct eight errors in the following paragraph:

Employeees need to dress appropriately every day of the week, no longer will friday be a casual day. Infact, customers have commented alot on the proffessional look of our sales team. Lets make sure that we keep up our our good work and good image.

117

0-7424-1807-3 Building Grammar & Writing Skills

Name _____ Date _____

Resumes

One of the first things you will want to do when you begin looking for a job is to create a resume, which is an itemized list of information about you that prospective employers would find useful. This list includes your education, part-time jobs you've had, hobbies and interests that might indicate your suitability for the job you are seeking, names of people who could verify that you are a responsible and capable worker, and information about where to contact you. As with all professional documents, it is essential that the resume be error free, indicating to the reader that you would take the same care with tasks on the job. The following model shows one way to include the information in neat, easy-to-see sections. Study the model; then create one of your own, using the model as your guide.

JOHN EDWARD McCLENNAN
121 South Woodrow Boulevard
Birch Cliff, IL 61799
Phone: 000-734-3333   **e-mail: jemclennan@aol.com**

OBJECTIVE   Part-time summer work in lawn care

EDUCATION
- Birch Cliff Junior High School, Birch Cliff, IL
- Will graduate in June 2003
- Perfect attendance during the past year

WORK EXPERIENCE
- Helped local farmers during hay season (summer 2002)
- Assumed complete care of family lawn last five years
- Mowed neighborhood lawns last two summers (2001, 2002)
- Familiar with operation of small and large mowers

HOBBIES AND INTERESTS
- Working on cars
- Carpentry and woodworking
- Playing guitar

REFERENCES

Mr. Ernie Peters	Ms. Sharon Barthelemy	Ms. Leda McLennan
Farmer	Neighbor	Language Arts Teacher
2709 N. 3502 Rd.	320 S. Woodrow	Birch Cliff Junior H. S.
Midland, IL 62784	Birch Cliff, IL 61799	Birch Cliff, IL 61799
(000-734-5873)	(000-734-9009)	(000-734-4983)

Write your own resume, using a word processor to make it professional looking. Have at least two people proofread it to make certain that you have made no errors.

       0-7424-1807-3 Building Grammar & Writing Skills

Name _____ Date _____

Resume Cover Letter

Along with your resume, you will want to send a job application cover letter each time you apply for a specific job. Read the following model cover letter, then answer the questions about the writer's purpose below.

May 15, 2003

Ms. Judy Garrison
404 South Woodrow Boulevard
Birch Cliff, IL 61799

Dear Ms. Garrison:

I have learned that my friend Robert James, who mowed your lawn last summer, has moved away and that you are looking for a new lawn care person.
I would like to apply for the job. I will be graduating from Birch Cliff Junior High the first week in June and will be available all summer.

As you will see in my resume, I have mowed lawns for the past two summers for neighbors in the area, and I have taken care of the yard for my family for the past five years. I also worked for Mr. Peters last summer, helping to put up hay. My experience working on cars and other machinery with my dad has helped me to be comfortable working with both small and large mowers.

The people I have listed on the resume have said they would speak to anyone who calls about my work. Mr. Peters can tell you about my work on his farm, Ms. Barthelemy will tell you about my work on her lawn last year, and Ms. McLennan will tell you about my work at school.

I will call you next week to see if you would be willing to interview me for the job.

Sincerely,

---

1. What is the point of paragraph 1? _____

2. What is the point of paragraph 2? _____

3. What is the point of paragraph 3? _____

4. What is the point of paragraph 4? _____

Based on the information in your resume, and following the model above, write a letter of application for a job you feel qualified to do, such as baby sitting, caring for pets, running errands, shoveling snow, or carrying newspapers. Make certain to ask for an interview.

0-7424-1807-3 Building Grammar & Writing Skills

Name _____ Date _____

Follow-Up Letter

If you have been successful in getting an interview, it is a good idea to follow up the interview with a thank you letter. In addition to being courteous, sending a letter may give you an edge if there has been more than one applicant for the job. The letter should be brief, sincere, and error free.

---

121 South Woodrow Boulevard
Birch Cliff, IL 61799
May 23, 2003

Ms. Judy Garrison
404 South Woodrow Boulevard
Birch Cliff, IL 61799

Dear Ms. Garrison:

Thank you for letting me talk to you today about taking care of your lawn this summer. I am happy that you think I will be able to handle the job.

When you gave me the tour of your yard, I was impressed by the nice gardens that you have. I intend to use the smaller mower and the weed eater to trim around the trees, flower gardens, and vegetable garden. The riding mower will be perfect for the large area of grass.

I will call you the first day that school is out to set up a work schedule.

Sincerely,

John McLennan

---

1. What is the point of paragraph 1? _____

2. What is the point of paragraph 2? _____

3. What is the point of paragraph 3? _____

Write a thank you letter for the "interview" that you had following your letter of application.

   0-7424-1807-3 Building Grammar & Writing Skills

Name _____ Date _____

Business Cards

To make your job search more effective, you may want to create business cards to pass out to prospective employers. As with your resume, you will want to give readers a clear and concise idea of what service you can perform and how they might reach you. Below is a sample business card highlighting information on the resume.

McLennan Lawn Care

121 South Woodrow Boulevard

Birch Cliff, IL 61799

Phone: 000-734-3333   jemclennan@aol.com

Farm Labor	John E. McLennan
Lawn Maintenance	5 Years Experience

In the space below, design your own business card, based on the resume that you created earlier.

0-7424-1807-3 Building Grammar & Writing Skills

Name _____ Date _____

E-mail Messages

Much of today's business communication is done by e-mail. Because e-mail seems less formal than a letter, it is tempting to send a note off quickly, without carefully checking what has been said. However, as with a formal letter, the recipient of an e-mail message has only the written words to judge both your attitude and the quality of your ideas. The danger of hitting the "send" button too quickly is that you cannot get it back. For all business e-mail, follow these guidelines:

- Use Standard English.
- Avoid all caps.
- Separate paragraphs with a blank line.
- Proofread carefully to be certain that your message is polite, clear, and error free.
- Do not trust spell check to find all spelling problems, such as typing *there* instead of *their*.

The e-mail below, while well-written, has several errors. Find at least four errors from the categories above, and list them on the lines below the e-mail.

To:	skethineni@univ.org
Subject:	Request for Interview

Dear Dr. Kethineni:

I am working for our local newspaper this summer on a career project about women in unusual professions. You're job as a university professor in the field of criminal justice would be interesting for our readers, and we would like to include an interview with you in our project. This information will be included in a back-to-school issue this fall.

If you are able to meet with me, I can be available whenever you have time. Please reply to me at e-mail address below. Thank you for considering this request.

Sincerely,

LOIS A. GUYON
laguyon@aol.com

1. _____   3. _____

2. _____   4. _____

Create an e-mail of your own following the above guidelines. Write to a friend or relative in another city, asking for information about that city to include in a school report.

   0-7424-1807-3 Building Grammar & Writing Skills

Name _____ Date _____

Project Reports

Employees in many types of occupations are called on to report on some aspect of their jobs. They may be working at a greenhouse and need to report on the types of fertilizer that have been used for various plants and their effectiveness, or they may be working in a factory where they need to report the numbers of bottles broken in the filling line and the reasons for the breakage. Usually these reports are delivered in writing, but often they are also delivered in oral reports. In the following section, you will create a written report, as well as gather materials for presentation of an oral report.

Generating the Information. Assume you are helping out at summer school, and school administrators have asked you to interview students to find out how they are enjoying their summer school experience. You create a survey asking students this question: "What is the best thing about summer school (*choose one*): subjects, teachers, extracurricular activities, or friends?" The students' responses list *friends* first, followed by *extracurricular activities, subjects,* and *teachers*.

Creating Visual Information. The administrator asks you to provide visual information with your report to show what you asked and what the students said. This is the chart you create.

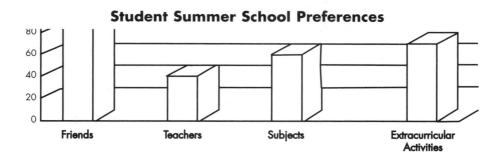

Student Summer School Preferences

1. Based on this chart, what would you say was the number of students surveyed? _____

2. How many reported *friends* as the most important thing in school? _____

3. What percent is this of the overall number of students surveyed? _____

4. How many reported *teachers*? _____   5. What is the percent? _____

6. How many reported *subjects*? _____   7. What is the percent? _____

8. How many reported *extracurricular activities*? _____   9. What is the percent? _____

10. What would your answer be if you were asked this question? _____

123

Name _____ Date _____

Write a Project Report

There are many ways a report can be formatted, but whatever style you use, you will want to follow some basic guidelines. Below is one style that is commonly used. Main headings are centered. Second-level headings are placed in the left margin. Visual information is important.

Student Attitudes About Summer School

Survey Question
Because summer school is a new addition this year at Jefferson Junior High, school administrators were interested in knowing how well students were enjoying it. They asked student workers to conduct a survey of 270 students, asking students what they enjoyed most about summer school: subjects, teachers, extracurricular activities, or friends. Students wrote their answers on survey sheets, which were collected and sorted.

Student Responses
Student preferences were as follows: 100 students (37%) named friends as the most important thing about summer school; 70 students (26%) said that extracurricular activities were the best; 60 students (22%) liked the subjects they were taking; and, 40 students (15%) said they liked teachers best.

Student Attitudes About Summer School

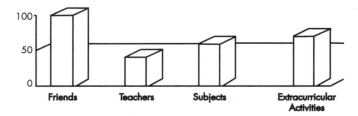

Conclusions
These responses show that students had a very positive attitude toward summer school. Not surprisingly, students enjoyed spending time with their friends most of all, with extracurricular activities second. These answers are probably not very different from what adults would say about their jobs and leisure activities. Although subjects and teachers were not the top winners, there were still a total of 100 students who chose either subjects or teachers as the best thing about summer school. The administration can be pleased that students are apparently enjoying their summer school experience.

Working in small groups, conduct your own survey of 20–25 people. Have each group select a survey question for the class to answer (favorite TV show, food, or sport, etc.). Show the results in a bar graph, and write a report, using the example above as a model.

Present your group's report to the class orally following the points in the written report and using a large graph as a visual aid.

124

Answer Key

Capitals Rule! (p. 9)
1. the first word in a sentence
2. people's names
3. titles (or book titles)
4. historical periods
5. cities and countries (or geographical locations)

Capital Etiquette (p. 10)
1. Actress Jennifer Anniston, Jennifer Anastassakis; She, Rachel
2. Andy Garcia; Information, I, Andres Arturo Garcia Menendez
3. One, Woody Allen; Born Allen Stewart Konigsberg, A.S.K.
4. Star, Meg Ryan; It, Miss Ryan; She, Margaret Mary Emily Anne Hyra

Of Uppercase Importance (p. 11)
Works of Art:	*Top Gun, Born on the Fourth of July, Mission Impossible*
Publications:	*Chicago Tribune, New York Times*
Companies:	Universal, Columbia Tri-Star, Paramount
Organizations:	Church of Scientology

We're Important Too! (p. 12)
1. Brussels, Belgium; October;
2. Winterset, Iowa; May; Academy Awards; 3. New York; November

Punctuation Eliminates Confusion (p. 15)
Student choices may vary and still be grammatically correct.
"Do you know," said Anne confidentially, "I've made up my mind to enjoy this drive. It's been my experience that you can nearly always enjoy things if you make up your mind firmly that you will. Of course, you must make it up FIRMLY. I am not going to think about going back to the asylum while we're having our drive. I'm just going to think about the drive. Oh, look, there's one little early wild rose out! Isn't it lovely? Don't you think it must be glad to be a rose? Wouldn't it be nice if roses could talk? I'm sure they could tell us such lovely things."

End Marks (p. 16)
1. question mark
2. period
3. exclamation point
4-6. Answers vary.

Comma: The In,ter,rupt,er (p. 17)
1. Karel, [who love to fish for Muskies],
2. plans, [unfortunately],
3. However,
4. At the first opportunity,
5. They will be on their way to the great waters of the North at the first opportunity.

Commas Give Us Pause (p. 18)
1. Saturday, March 22, 2003, in Ottawa, Illinois.
2. November 20, 1938, in Toronto, Ontario, Canada.

Cordial and Carried Away Commas (p. 19)
1. C   2. W   3. W

He Agrees That We Agree (p. 23)
Sentences will vary;
sample sentences follow.
1. St. Louis and Kansas City lie west of the Mississippi River. (are)
2. The editor with his three assistants suggests ways to improve. (is)
3. The girls and their brother enjoy swimming. (are)
4. Either Jason or the twins volunteer at the library on Tuesday evenings. (are)
5. Golf or bowling challenges both novices and veterans. (is)
6. Neither the houses nor the apartment building offers enough room. (is)
7. The athletes on the team work hard during practice. (are)
8. A poem, a fable, and an essay appear in my portfolio. (are)
9. Two cantaloupe or one watermelon feeds our family. (is)
10. Several novels and poems interest young children. (are)

Everybody Agrees, But Few Concur (p. 24)
Sentences will vary;
sample sentences follow.
1. Both begin class at 8:00 A.M. (were)
2. Everyone studies for weekly vocabulary quizzes. (was)
3. Some of the milk spills whenever Jessie pours it. (was)
4. Some of the glasses break easily. (were)
5. Many of the assignments include multiple steps. (were)
6. None of the sand contains pebbles. (was)
7. Few of her errors cause confusion. (were)
8. No one leaves before finishing dessert. (was)
9. None of David's story causes the reader to laugh. (was)
10. None of David's sentences contain punctuation errors. (were)

Adjectives and Adverbs Add Detail (p. 25)
Sentences will vary;
sample sentences follow.
2. Tara answered the question quickly and decisively.
3. Carefully and slowly, Samantha reread her essay.
4. The tall, dark man lumbered down the street with his cloak flowing.
5. The visitor, flamboyant and daring, walked down the street at midnight.

Verb Phrases (p. 26)
1. was working   2. had written
3. had lived   4. will read
5. does write   6. is writing
7. will be revising 8. will edit

Participial Phrases (p. 28)
Sentences will vary;
sample sentences follow.
2. Jayne, finding her CDs broken, blamed her brother.
3. The man crossing the street avoided the St. Bernard.
4. Enjoying her first circus, the child laughed at the clown's antics.
5. Raising her arms into the air, Samantha crossed the finish line first.
6. Known for its helpful citizens, our town is a great place to live.

© McGraw-Hill Children's Publishing   0-7424-1807-3 Building Grammar & Writing Skills

Answer Key

Independent Clauses (p. 29)
Sentences will vary;
sample sentences follow.
1. S   Thirty major league baseball stadiums currently exist.
2. C   Fenway Park in Boston, Massachusetts, is the oldest, and Wrigley Field in Chicago, Illinois, is the second oldest.
3. C   Qualcomm Stadium in San Diego, California, has the largest capacity; it holds over 65,000 fans.
4. S   Qualcomm Stadium was previously called Jack Murphy Stadium.
5. C   Minute Maid, Comerica, and Pacific Bell are three fairly new parks; they all opened in 2000.
6. S   Play began on April 6, 2001, at PNC Park and on April 9, 2001, at Miller Park.
7. S   Have you seen Olympic Stadium in Montreal or the Sky Dome in Toronto?

Dependent Clauses: Adjective (p. 30)
Sentences will vary;
sample sentences follow.
1. Samuel Langhorne Clemens, who lived in Hannibal, Missouri, from 1839 to 1853, is better known as Mark Twain.
2. Many characters in *The Adventures of Tom Sawyer* are based upon people that Twain knew when he lived in Hannibal.
3. Among characters based on people is Tom whose character was created from characteristics of two friends and from parts of Twain himself.
4. Mark Twain created another memorable character, Becky Thatcher, who was based on a family neighbor.
5. The cave, which appears in the novel, is most likely based on McDowell's cave in Hannibal, Missouri.
6. Mark Twain may have included the cave in his book after he read a newspaper article that appeared in the *St. Louis Democrat* in the spring of 1874.
7. William Dean Howells, from whom Twain received advice, was a fellow author and friend.

Dependent Clauses: Adverb (p. 31)
Sentences will vary; sample sentences follow.
1. Although many strategies exist to help students, they often have problems with the writing process.
2. If the assignment or deadline is not due soon, writers may put the draft away for a period of time.
3. Many professional writers write much more than they use since they find it easier to delete unimportant "extra" information rather than to think of new material.
4. Before they submit their work to publishers, many professional writers ask trusted friends to read their drafts and give advice.
5. Although writing every day seems rigorous, nearly every professional author follows a daily writing routine.
6. Beginning writers will likely find the above strategies beneficial when they experience difficulty finishing a writing assignment.

Know Your Nouns (p. 33)
1. thing 2. person 3. person 4. place
5. idea 6. thing 7. place
8. person 9. person 10. thing
1. Penguins, seabirds, humans
2. legs
3. Scientists, penguins, humans
4. feathers, layer, fat, cold
5. Penguins, New Zealand, Australia, South Africa
6. curiosity, penguins, creatures
7. penguins, time, eggs, land
8. penguin, egg, male
9. penguins, zoo
10. Antarctica

Types of Nouns (p. 34)
1. (a) writers–common,
   (b) inspiration–abstract
2. (a) Jack London–proper,
   (b) stories–common
3. (a) audience–collective/common,
   (b) boyhood–compound/common
4. (a) Yukon–proper,
   (b) gold–common/concrete
5. (a) success–abstract,
   (b) experiences–common
6. (a) *The Call of the Wild*–compound/proper,
   (b) pack–collective/common

Functions of Nouns (p. 35)
1. Students (7), session (2), memories (4)
2. writers (1), events (2), reactions (4)
3. places (2), patterns (4), characters (4)
4. employment (3), jobs (6)
5. Mark Twain (1), pilot (3), mill (4)
6. dreams (6), writers (5), category (2)
7. *Frankenstein* (6), nightmare (4)
8. minutes (2), students (7), experiences (4)

Become Pronoun Pros (p. 36)
Sentences will vary but should include the following pronouns:
1. he   2. our/ours   3. you
4. me   5. him   6. your/yours
7. us   8. her/hers

Who Knows These Pronouns? (p. 37)
1. What   2. herself
3. themselves   4. This
5. that   6. What
7. himself   8. themselves
9. Who   10. Those

Verbs: Regular and Irregular (p. 38)
delete deleted have/has/had deleted
revise revised have/has/had revised
finish finished have/has/had finished
create created have/has/had created
see   saw   have/has/had seen
write   wrote   have/has/had written
go   went   have/has/had gone
bring   brought have/has/had brought
burst   burst   have/has/had burst
make   made   have/has/had made

Adjectives Describe or Limit (p. 40)
1. 1831 (5), a (1), her (3)
2. prewriting (9), English (7)
3. three (5), best (10)
4. that (2), miserable (6)
5. terrifying (9), apparent (10), her (3)
6. Which (4)
7. great (10), to read (8)

Adverbs Anywhere and Everywhere (p. 41)
1. intently (A)
2. Even (E), now (B)
3. why (D), how (A)
4. very (E)
5. extremely (E), too (E)
6. unusually (E), far (C)
7. finally (B), there (C), bravely (A)
8. everywhere (C), then (B), loudly (A)
9. soundly (A)
10. Nowadays (B), soon (B)

© McGraw-Hill Children's Publishing   0-7424-1807-3 Building Grammar & Writing Skills

Answer Key

Prepositions Like Company (p. 42)
1. <u>about</u> paper currency–ADV
2. <u>in</u> 1913–ADV
3. <u>Under</u> federal law–ADV, <u>of</u> the Treasury–ADJ, <u>in</u> many denominations–ADJ
4. <u>with</u> red and blue fibers–ADJ, <u>for</u> paper currency–ADV
5. <u>with</u> many digits–ADJ, <u>on</u> all paper money–ADV
6. <u>of</u> 18 months–ADJ
7. <u>from</u> 1794–ADV, <u>to</u> 1935–ADV

Conjunctions and Interjections, Oh My! (p. 43)
1. Neither, nor
2. but
3. Wow! (circled), both, and
4. but
5. Since
6. neither, nor
7. and

Generating Ideas (p. 45)
Answers may vary. Possible responses:
1. Talked friends into stealing stones to build a wharf
2. Leadership ability
3. Nothing is useful that is not honest.

Creating Titles and Headings (p. 58)
Answers may vary.
Section 1: Nonfiction
Section 2: Fiction
Section 3: Poetry
Section 4: Drama

Writing Outlines (p. 60)
Title: Ways to Eliminate Stress
I. Organize
  A. Clean locker
  B. Rearrange folders
  C. Make lists of due dates
    1. Assignments
    2. Quizzes and tests
    3. Other obligations
II. Exercise
  A. Aerobic
    1. Swimming
    2. Jogging
  B. Anaerobic
    1. Yoga
    2. Weight lifting

Quotations in Narrative Writing (p. 64)
It all came about one day when my mom asked, "Would you boys like to take a ride?"

"Sure," we said. "Where are we going?"

"We're going to run the lawn mower to the shop for repairs," my mother replied.

"Mom, is it okay if Aaron and I get a maze book and some treats on the way?"

"Well, okay, and you better pick up a package of pencils too."

Quotations in Expository Writing (p. 65)
1. Mary Peters
2. According to Mary Peters
3. 14
4. Ann Karel
5. Ann Karel, a noted Dickens researcher, says,
6. 7

Polishing the Visual Appearance (p. 85)
Solutions may vary.
Possible poem format:
I want to be your friend
Forever and ever without break or decay.
When the hills are all flat
And the rivers are all dry
When it lightens and thunders in winter
When it rains and snows in summer
When heaven and earth mingle
Not till then will I part from you.

Chronological Sequence (p. 87)
The order of the events follows:
2, 1, 3, 6, 5, 9, 4, 10, 7, 8, 12, 11

Short Fiction: Chinese Fables (p. 95)
Answers may vary. Possible theme statements: "Suspicion": People's prejudices or snap judgments cause them to inappropriately interpret other people's behavior. "Short Sightedness": People often want to appear better or more knowledgeable than they are and, in so doing, make themselves appear far worse.

Visual Images: The Novel (p. 96)
1. Answers will vary.
2. birds, prairie dog, rabbits, coyotes
3. long grass, cabbage stalks, hedgerows, trees

Formal Responses to Literature (pp. 97–98)
Answers may vary. Possible responses:
1. Mrs. Johnson dreams of success and fame for herself and her family. Her daughter Dee becomes successful, but shallow, living in her own fantasy world. Dee's sister Maggie, who is disfigured and not successful by her sister's standards, leads a simple and happy life. Mrs. Johnson eventually sees that Maggie's life and values are more desirable.
2. "What Dee and her Mother really value—in sharp contrast to their dreams—is the lives they already lead: their "everyday lives" (paragraph 1). A person's real, everyday life, is better than a dream (paragraph 5).
3. Yes. In paragraph 1, she says that Dee and her mother are "like many people who have dreams and wishes" and "envision worlds that hold the promise of wonderful lives. However, these dreams do not reflect the real desires of the dreamers."

Analyzing Persuasive Techniques (p. 100)
Answers may vary. Possible responses:
1. Advertisers target children because they influence parents to buy, and they believe what they hear. The advertising industry needs to set up guidelines to control this unethical behavior.
2. Advertising is not harmful to children, parents need to teach children about advertising, schools need to teach children to be wiser consumers, and most companies are responsible.
3. Advertisers ignore research on dangers because they want to make money; children watch a lot of television; parents are too busy to monitor everything; advertisers use music and famous people to keep children's attention and make them believe the advertisements; children don't understand the difference between programs and advertisements; and children pressure parents into buying.
4. Advertisers need to stop blaming others and accept responsibility for monitoring the quality of advertising on children's programs. Everyone will benefit.

0-7424-1807-3 Building Grammar & Writing Skills

Answer Key

5. Purpose: to persuade the advertising industry to become more responsible
6. Audience: members of the advertising industry, parents.
7. The industry would care about losing money; the parents care about their children
8–11. Opinions will vary

Take Notes from Secondary Sources (p. 107)
1. Dental assistants work in
2. page 309
3. #2
4. Outlook
5. page 101
6. #4

Write the Paper (p. 111)
Students' Words:
Thirty years ago the term "Webmaster" did not exist. Today, because of growth of the Internet, the term Webmaster has become commonplace.

Source information #1:
Webmasters oversee "every aspect of a Web site. They study issues such as accessibility and approve information that appears on the site." (62) Quotation

Source information #2:
Webmasters place a high priority on accessibility for clients since time is so very important in the workplace. (287) Paraphrase

Source information #3:
"Webmasters do not actually create content for the Web site but approve or reject the information and design that has been already created." (71) Quotation

Identify Sources (p. 112)
Edward Kinman, a career counselor
Dennis Gomez
Robert Watson, president of Career Placement, Inc.

Introductory Tags
says
According to
agrees, saying,

Create a Works Cited Page (p. 114)
Pasternak, Ceel, and Linda Thornburg. "Wildlife Management." *Cool Careers for Girls with Animals*. Manassas Park, Virginia: Impact Publications, Inc., 1999. 49–56.

Quinlan, Kathryn A. *Careers Without College: Makeup Artist*. Mankato, Minnesota: Capstone Books, 1999.

Woodward, Kevin. "More Than a Pill Counter." *Quincy-Herald Whig* 26 September 2002: A7.

General Guidelines (p. 117)
1. minister, 4-H Club, librarian, school board, sales clerk, principal
2. to explain a process, to report results, to ask for help
3. order of importance, chronological sequence
4. Guidelines for Professional Appearance
5. <u>Employees</u> need to dress appropriately every day of the <u>week.</u> <u>No</u> longer will <u>Friday</u> be a casual day. <u>In fact</u>, customers have commented <u>a lot</u> on the <u>professional</u> look of our <u>sales</u> team. <u>Let's</u> make sure that we keep up our good work and
good image.

Resume Cover Letter (p. 119)
Answers may vary. Possible answers:
1. Why John is writing
2. What his qualifications are
3. What references will tell them
4. To ask for an interview

Follow-Up Letter (p. 120)
1. Thank Ms. Garrison for the interview
2. Tell Ms. Garrison how the work will be done
3. Set up a work schedule.

E-mail Messages (p. 122)
1. <u>You're</u> should be *your*
2. <u>at e-mail address</u> should be *at the e-mail address*
3. separate paragraphs beginning with "<u>If you are able</u>" and "<u>Thank you</u>"
4. LOIS A. GUYON should be Lois A. Guyon

Project Reports (p. 123)
1. 270
2. 100
3. 37%
4. 40
5. 15%
6. 60
7. 22%
8. 70
9. 26%

0-7424-1807-3 Building Grammar & Writing Skills